Apple Inc.

A Case Study for Lewis University
Romeoville, IL

Strategic Management and the Global Environment

By:

Roscoe Myrmingos
Adam Bancroft
George Kamba
Mark Veselsky
David Kelnhofer

Table of Contents

I. Diagnosis
    A. Mission……………………………………………………………………………….4

    B. Objectives……………………………………………………………………………..4

    C. Corporate Strategy……………………………………………………………………4

    D. Policies………………………………………………………………………………..6

        1. Diversity……………………………………………………………………..6

        2. Ethical Standards/Code of Business Conduct……………………………….6

        3. Suppliers……………………………………………………………………14

        4. Human Resources…………………………………………………………..14

    E. Strategic Managers and Board of Directors………………………………………….15

        1. Senior Level Executives……………………………………………………15

        2. Corporate Governance……………………………………………………..21

            a. Board Member Responsibilities……………………………………21

            b. Board Committees…………………………………………………22

            c. Director Compensation……………………………………………..24

    F. Generic Industry Type………………………………………………………………..25

    G. Organization structure……………………………………………………………….46

        1. Advantages & Disadvantages………………………………………………47

    H. Financial Analysis……………………………………………………………………47

        1. Graphs……………………………………………………………………...48

        2. Altman Z-Score Analysis………………………………………………….61

      3. Tobin's Q & DuPont Analysis……………………………………………………62

I. SWOT Analysis……………………………………………………………………...68

    1. Strengths……………………………………………………………………69

    2. Weaknesses………………………………………………………………..74

    3. Opportunities………………………………………………………………76

    4. Threats……………………………………………………………………...79

        a. Tows Matrix……………………………………………………….82

II. Focal Points for Action……………………………………………………………...85

    A. Short Range………………………………………………………………...85

    B. Long Range………………………………………………………………...85

III. Develop Alternatives………………………………………………………………..85

    A. Generic Industry Type & Industry Characteristics……………………….85

    B. Boston Consulting Group Matrix………………………………………….86

    C. Competitive Position……………………………………………………….87

    D. Competitive Strategy Options……………………………………………..89

    E. Rumelt's Criteria…………………………………………………………...94

IV. Decisions & Recommendations…………………………………………………...95

    A. Corporate…………………………………………………………………...95

    B. Business……………………………………………………………………96

    C. Functional………………………………………………………………….97

V. Implementation……………………………………………………………………...98

VI. Citations……………………………………………………………………………100

I. Diagnosis

A. Mission

"It is Apple's mission to help transform the way people work, learn and communicate by providing exceptional computing and innovative customer service. We will pioneer new directions and approaches finding innovative ways to use computing technology to extend the bounds of human potential. Apple will make a difference: our products, services and insights will help people around the world shape the ways business and education will be done in the 21st century." Apple's mission statement details its strategic position to achieve profitability and the competitive advantage. Apple's strategic position is to give users the best computing experience by innovating in hardware, software, and Internet offerings."

B. Objectives

- Apple Inc. plans to keep creating and releasing computers and consumer electronics that are more user-friendly.
- Apple Inc. will focus more opening more stores domestically and in international locations to help increase in sales.
- Apple Inc. will increase our revenues 5% to 7% in five years.
- Apple Inc. wants to keep a good reputation.
- Apple Inc. continues to expand toward new media markets

C. Corporate Strategy

"The Company is committed to bringing the best personal computing, mobile communication and portable digital music and video experience to consumers, students, educators, businesses, and government agencies through its innovative hardware, software, peripherals, services, and Internet offerings. The Company's business strategy leverages its unique ability to design and develop its own operating system, hardware, application software, and services to provide its customers new products and solutions with superior ease-of-use, seamless integration, and innovative industrial design. The Company believes continual investment in research and development is critical to the development and enhancement of innovative products and technologies. In addition to evolving its personal computers and related solutions, the Company continues to capitalize on the convergence of the personal computer, mobile communications and digital consumer electronics by creating and refining innovations, such as iPhone, iPod and the iTunes Store. The Company desires to support a community for the development of third-party products that complement the Company's offerings through its developer programs. The Company offers various third-party software applications and hardware accessories for Mac ® computers, iPhones and iPods through its retail and online stores, as well as software applications for the iPhone and iPod touch platforms through its App Store™. The Company's strategy also includes expanding its distribution network to effectively reach more of its targeted customers and provide them with a high-quality sales and post-sales support experience.

Consumer and Small and Mid-Sized Business
The Company believes a high-quality buying experience with knowledgeable salespersons who can convey the value of the Company's products and services greatly enhances its ability to attract and retain customers. The Company sells many of its products and resells certain third-party products in most of its major markets directly to consumers and businesses through its retail and online stores. The Company has also invested in programs to enhance reseller sales, including the Apple Sales Consultant Program, which places Apple employees and contractors at selected third-party reseller locations, and the Apple Premium Reseller Program, through which independently run businesses focus on the Apple platform and provide a high level of customer service and product expertise. The Company believes providing direct contact with its targeted customers is an efficient way to demonstrate the advantages of its products over those of its competitors.

At the end of fiscal 2009, the Company had opened a total of 273 retail stores, including 217 stores in the U.S. and 56 stores internationally. The Company has typically located its stores at high-traffic locations in quality shopping malls and urban shopping districts. By operating its own stores and locating them in desirable high-traffic locations, the Company is better positioned to control the customer buying experience and attract new customers. The stores are designed to simplify and enhance the presentation and marketing of the Company's products and related solutions. To that end, retail store configurations have evolved into various sizes to accommodate market-specific demands. The stores employ experienced and knowledgeable personnel who provide product advice, service and training. The stores offer a wide selection of third-party hardware, software, and various other accessories and peripherals that complement the Company's products.

Education
Throughout its history, the Company has focused on the use of technology in education and has been committed to delivering tools to help educators teach and students learn. The Company believes effective integration of technology into classroom instruction can result in higher levels of student achievement, especially when used to support collaboration, information access, and the expression and representation of student thoughts and ideas. The Company has designed a range of products and services to address the needs of education

customers, which includes one-to-one ("1:1") learning. A 1:1 learning solution typically consists of a networked environment that includes a portable computer for every student and teacher. In addition, the Company supports mobile learning and real-time distribution and accessibility of education related materials through iTunes U, which allows students and teachers to share and distribute educational media directly through their computers and mobile communication devices.

Enterprise, Government and Creative
The Company also sell its hardware and software products to customers in enterprise, government and creative markets in each of its geographic segments. These markets are also important to many third-party developers who provide Mac-compatible hardware and software solutions. Customers in these markets utilize the Company's products because of their high-powered computing performance and expansion capabilities, networking functionality, and seamless integration with complementary products. The Company designs its high-end hardware solutions, including Mac Pro desktops, MacBook ® Pro and MacBook Air® portable systems, and Xserve® servers, to incorporate the power, expandability, and other features desired by these professionals. The Company's operating system, Mac OS® X, incorporates powerful graphics and audio technologies and features developer tools to optimize system and application performance."
(10-K, Apple, Inc.)

D. Policies

1. Diversity

Apple is committed to diversity. Apple is an equal opportunity employer and an affirmative action employer.

2. Ethical Standards/Code of Business Conduct

Labor and Human Rights
Suppliers must uphold the human rights of workers, and treat them with dignity and respect as understood by the international community.

Antidiscrimination
Suppliers shall not discriminate against any worker based on race, color, age, gender, sexual orientation, ethnicity, disability, religion, political affiliation, union membership, national origin, or marital status in hiring and employment practices such as applications for employment, promotions, rewards, access to training, job assignments, wages, benefits, discipline, and termination. Suppliers shall not require a pregnancy test or discriminate against pregnant workers except where required by applicable laws or regulations or prudent for workplace

safety. In addition, Suppliers shall not require workers or potential workers to undergo medical tests that could be used in a discriminatory way except where required by applicable law or regulation or prudent for workplace safety.

Fair Treatment

Suppliers shall commit to a workplace free of harassment. Suppliers shall not threaten workers with or subject them to harsh or inhumane treatment, including sexual harassment, sexual abuse, corporal punishment, mental coercion, physical coercion, verbal abuse or unreasonable restrictions on entering or exiting company provided facilities. Suppliers shall prohibit harassment and unlawful discrimination in the workplace.

Prevention of Involuntary Labor

Suppliers shall not use any form of forced, bonded, indentured, or prison labor. All work must be voluntary and workers shall be free to leave work or terminate their employment with reasonable notice. Workers must not be required to surrender any government-issued identification, passports, or work permits as a condition of employment. Suppliers shall ensure that third party agencies providing workers to Supplier are compliant with the provisions of the Code and the laws of the sending and receiving countries, whichever is more stringent in its protection of workers. Suppliers shall ensure that contracts for both direct and contract workers clearly convey the conditions of employment in a language understood by the worker. Where workers are required to pay a fee in connection with obtaining employment, Suppliers shall be responsible for payment of all fees and expenses in excess of the amount of one month of the worker's anticipated net wages. Such fees and expenses include, but are not limited to expenses associated with recruitment, processing or placement of both direct and contract Workers.

Prevention of Under Age Labor

Child labor is strictly prohibited. Suppliers shall not employ children. The minimum age for employment or work shall be 15 years of age, the minimum age for employment in that country, or the age for completing compulsory education in that country, whichever is higher. This Code does not prohibit participation in legitimate workplace apprenticeship programs that are consistent with Article 6 of ILO Minimum Age Convention No. 138 or light work consistent with Article 7 of ILO Minimum Age Convention No. 138.

Juvenile Worker Protections

Suppliers may employ juveniles who are older than the applicable legal minimum age for employment but are younger than 18 years of age, provided they do not perform work likely to

Apple Inc

jeopardize their health, safety, or morals, consistent with ILO Minimum Age Convention No. 138.

Working Hours

Except in emergency or unusual situations, a workweek shall be restricted to 60 hours, including overtime, and workers shall take at least one day off every seven-days.
All overtime shall be voluntary. Under no circumstances shall workweeks exceed the maximum permitted under applicable laws and regulations.

Wages and Benefits

Suppliers shall pay all workers at least the minimum wage required by applicable laws and regulations and provide all legally mandated benefits. In addition to their compensation for regular hours of work, workers shall be compensated for overtime hours at the premium rate required by applicable laws and regulations.
Suppliers shall not use deductions from wages as a disciplinary measure.
Suppliers shall offer vacation time, leave periods, and holidays consistent with applicable laws and regulations.
Suppliers shall pay workers in a timely manner and clearly convey the basis on which workers are being paid.

Freedom of Association

Suppliers must respect the right of workers to associate freely, form and join workers organizations of their own choosing, seek representation, and bargain collectively, as permitted by and in accordance with applicable laws and regulations. Suppliers shall not discriminate with respect to employment based on union membership and, in particular, shall not make employment subject to the condition that the worker relinquish union membership or agree not to join a union or cause the dismissal of or otherwise prejudice a worker by reason of union membership or participation in union activities outside working hours (or within working hours if the Supplier has consented to such activities or if required by applicable law or regulation). Suppliers shall protect against acts of interference with the establishment, functioning, or administration of workers' organizations in accordance with applicable laws and regulations.

Health and Safety

Apple recognizes that integrating sound health and safety management practices into all aspects of business is essential to maintain high morale and produce innovative products. Suppliers shall commit to creating safe working conditions and a healthy work environment for

Apple Inc

all of their workers.

Occupational Injury Prevention
Suppliers shall eliminate physical hazards where possible. Where physical hazards cannot be eliminated, Suppliers shall provide appropriate engineering controls such as physical guards, interlocks, and barriers. Where appropriate engineering controls are not possible, Suppliers shall establish appropriate administrative controls such as safe work procedures. In all cases, Suppliers shall provide workers with appropriate personal protective equipment. Workers shall not be disciplined for raising safety concerns and shall have the right to refuse unsafe working conditions without fear of reprisal until management adequately addresses their concerns.

Prevention of Chemical Exposure
Suppliers shall identify, evaluate, and control worker exposure to hazardous chemical, biological, and physical agents. Suppliers must eliminate chemical hazards where possible. Where chemical hazards cannot be eliminated, Suppliers shall provide appropriate engineering controls such as closed systems and ventilation. Where appropriate engineering controls are not possible, Suppliers shall establish appropriate administrative controls such as safe work procedures. In all cases, Suppliers shall provide workers with appropriate personal protective equipment.

Emergency Prevention, Preparedness, and Response
Suppliers shall anticipate, identify, and assess emergency situations and events and minimize their impact by implementing emergency plans and response procedures, including emergency reporting, worker notification and evacuation procedures, worker training and drills, appropriate first-aid supplies, appropriate fire detection and suppression equipment, adequate exit facilities, and recovery plans. Suppliers shall incorporate C-TPAT security criteria into their business processes as described in the U.S. Customs website, www.cbp.gov.

Occupational Safety Procedures and Systems
Suppliers shall establish procedures and systems to manage, track, and report occupational injury and illness. Such procedures and systems shall encourage worker reporting, classify and record injury and illness cases, investigate cases and implement corrective actions to eliminate their causes, provide necessary medical treatment, and facilitate the workers' return to work.

Apple Inc

Ergonomics
Suppliers shall identify, evaluate, and control worker exposure to physically demanding tasks, including manual material handling, heavy lifting, prolonged standing, and highly repetitive or forceful assembly tasks.

Dormitory and Dining
Suppliers shall provide workers with clean toilet facilities, access to potable water, and sanitary food preparation and storage facilities. Worker dormitories provided by the Supplier or a third party agency shall be clean and safe and provide adequate emergency egress, adequate heat and ventilation, reasonable personal space, and reasonable entry and exit privileges.

Health and Safety Communication
In order to foster a safe work environment, Suppliers shall provide workers with appropriate workplace health and safety information and training, including written health and safety information and warnings, in the primary language of the workers. Suppliers shall post, in the primary language of its workers, Material Safety Data Sheets for any hazardous or toxic substances used in the workplace and properly train workers who will come into contact with such substances in the workplace.

Worker Health and Safety Committees
Suppliers are encouraged to initiate and support worker health and safety committees to enhance ongoing health and safety education and to encourage worker input regarding health and safety issues in the workplace.

Environmental Impact
At Apple, environmental considerations are an integral part of our business practices. Suppliers shall commit to reducing the environmental impact of their designs, manufacturing processes, and waste emissions.

Hazardous Substance Management and Restrictions
Suppliers shall comply with the most recent version of Apple's Regulated Substances Specification, 069-0135 and with any applicable laws and regulations prohibiting or restricting the use or handling of specific substances. To ensure safe handling, movement, storage, recycling, reuse, and disposal, Suppliers shall identify and manage substances that pose a hazard if released to the environment and comply with applicable labeling laws and regulations for recycling and disposal.

Apple Inc

Solid Waste Management
Suppliers shall manage and dispose of non-hazardous solid waste generated from operations as required by applicable laws and regulations.

Wastewater and Storm water Management
Suppliers shall monitor, control, and treat wastewater generated from operations before discharge as required by applicable laws and regulations. Supplier shall take appropriate precautions to prevent contamination of storm water runoff from its facilities.

Air Emissions Management
Supplier shall characterize, monitor, control and treat air emissions of volatile organic chemicals, aerosols, corrosives, particulates, ozone depleting chemicals, and combustion byproducts generated from operations, as required by applicable laws and regulations, before discharge.

Environmental Permits and Reporting
Suppliers must obtain, maintain, and keep current all required environmental permits (e.g. discharge monitoring) and registrations and follow the operational and reporting requirements of such permits.

Pollution Prevention and Resource Reduction
Suppliers must endeavor to reduce or eliminate solid waste, wastewater and air emissions, including energy-related indirect air emissions, by implementing appropriate conservation measures in their production, maintenance and facilities processes, and by recycling, re-using, or substituting materials.

Ethics
Suppliers must be committed to the highest standards of ethical conduct when dealing with workers, suppliers, and customers.

Business Integrity
Corruption, extortion, and embezzlement, in any form, are strictly prohibited. Suppliers shall not violate the Foreign Corrupt Practices Act (FCPA), any international anti-corruption conventions, and applicable anti-corruption laws and regulations of the countries in which they operate, and shall not engage in corruption, extortion or embezzlement in any form. Suppliers shall not offer or accept bribes or other means to obtain an undue or improper advantage. Suppliers must uphold fair business standards in advertising, sales, and competition.

Apple Inc

Disclosure of Information

Suppliers must accurately record and disclose information regarding their business activities, structure, financial situation, and performance in accordance with applicable laws and regulations and prevailing industry practices.

Whistleblower Protection and Anonymous Complaints

Suppliers shall create programs to ensure the protection of Supplier and worker whistleblower confidentiality and prohibit retaliation against workers who participate in such programs in good faith or refuse an order that is in violation of the Apple Supplier Code of Conduct. Suppliers shall provide an anonymous complaint mechanism for workers to report workplace grievances in accordance with local laws and regulations.

Community Engagement

Suppliers are encouraged to engage the community to help foster social and economic development and to contribute to the sustainability of the communities in which they operate.

Protection of Intellectual Property

Suppliers must respect intellectual property rights; safeguard customer information; and transfer of technology and know-how must be done in a manner that protects intellectual property rights.

Management Commitment

Suppliers must adopt or establish a management system designed to ensure compliance with this Code and applicable laws and regulations, identify and mitigate related operational risks, and facilitate continuous improvement. ISO 14001, OHSAS 18001, Eco Management and Audit System (EMAS) may be useful resources. The management commitment should contain the following elements:

Company Statement

a corporate social and environmental responsibility statement affirming the Supplier's commitment to compliance and continual improvement, to be posted in the primary local language at all of the Supplier's worksites.
Management Accountability and Responsibility
clearly identified company representatives responsible for ensuring implementation and periodic review of the status of the Supplier's management systems.

Risk Assessment and Management

A process to identify environmental, health and safety, business ethics, labor, human

Apple Inc

rights, and legal compliance risks associated with their operations, determine the relative significance of each risk, and implement appropriate procedures and physical controls to ensure compliance and control the identified risks. Risk assessments for health and safety must include warehouse and storage facilities, plant and facility support equipment, laboratories and test areas, bathrooms, kitchens, cafeterias, and worker housing.

Performance Objectives with Implementation Plans and Measures
Written standards, performance objectives, targets, and implementation plans, including a periodic assessment of the Supplier's performance against those objectives.

Audits and Assessments
Periodic self-evaluations to ensure that the Supplier, its subcontractors and its next-tier Suppliers are complying with this Code and with applicable laws and regulations.

Documentation and Records
Supplier shall have processes to identify, monitor, and understand applicable laws and regulations and the additional requirements imposed by this Code. Supplier shall obtain, maintain and keep current a valid business license as required by applicable laws and regulations.
Creation of documents and records to ensure regulatory compliance and conformity to this Code, with appropriate confidentiality measures to protect privacy.

Training and Communication
Programs for training managers and workers to implement the Supplier's policies and procedures and fulfill Supplier's improvement objectives.

A process for communicating clear and accurate information about the Supplier's performance, practices, and expectations to its workers, suppliers, and customers.

Worker Feedback and Participation
An ongoing process to obtain feedback on processes and practices related to this Code and to foster continuous improvement.

Corrective Action Process
A process for timely correction of any deficiencies identified by an internal or external audit,

assessment, inspection, investigation, or review.
("Apple Supplier Code of Conduct", Apple, Inc.)

3. Suppliers

Apple Supplier Code of Conduct

"Apple is committed to ensuring that working conditions in Apple's supply chain are safe, that workers are treated with respect and dignity, and that manufacturing processes are environmentally responsible. Apple's suppliers ("Suppliers") commit, in all of their activities, to operate in full compliance with the laws, rules, and regulations of the countries in which they operate. This Supplier Code of Conduct ("Code") goes further, drawing upon internationally recognized standards, in order to advance social and environmental responsibility.

Apple requires that Suppliers implement this Code using the management systems described below. Apple may visit (and/or have external monitors visit) Supplier facilities, with or without notice, to assess compliance with this Code and to audit Supplier's wage, hour, payroll, and other worker records and practices. Violations of this Code may result in immediate termination as an Apple Supplier and in legal action. The Apple Supplier Code of Conduct is modeled on and contains language from the Electronic Industry Code of Conduct. Recognized standards such as the Universal Declaration of Human Rights (UDHR), and standards issued by organizations such as the International Labor Organization (ILO), Social Accountability International (SAI), and the Ethical Trading Initiative (ETI) were used as references in preparing this Code and may be useful sources of additional information. A complete list of references is provided at the end of this Code. As an extension of the Code, Apple maintains a series of detailed Standards that clarify our expectations for compliance."

("Apple Supplier Code of Conduct", Apple, Inc., Page 1)

4. Human Resources

Human Resources are responsible for recruiting and developing the best and brightest employees in every division, and supporting them throughout their careers. From benefits to training to employee relations, HR keeps our valued team members happy so that they can keep Apple one step ahead of the competition.

E. Strategic Managers and Board of Directors

1. Senior Level Executives

Steven P. Jobs
Chief Executive Officer
Since: 1997
Compensation: 1 USD

Mr. Jobs has been the CEO at Apple since 1997. He is one of the company's co-founders. Mr. Jobs also has been a Director at the Walt Disney since 2006. He is also one of the co-founders of Pixar Animation Studios, which merged with Walt Disney in 2006.

Timothy D. Cook
Chief Operating Officer
Compensation: 14,001,040 USD

Mr. Cook is the Chief Operating Officer of Apple. He joined the company in 1998. He also served with the company as the Executive Vice President, Worldwide Sales and Operations from 2002 to 2005, as the Senior Vice President, Worldwide Operations, Sales, Service and Support from 2000 to 2002, and as the Senior Vice President, Worldwide Operations from 1998 to 2000. Prior to joining the company, Mr. Cook held the position of Vice President, Corporate Materials at Compaq Computer (Compaq). Previous to his work at Compaq, he was the Chief Operating Officer of the Reseller Division at Intelligent Electronics. Mr. Cook also spent 12 years with IBM, most recently serving as Director of North American Fulfillment. He also serves as a member of the Board of Directors at Nike and the National Football Foundation.

Jeff Williams
Senior Vice President, Operations
Since: 1998
Compensation:

Jeff joined Apple in 1998 as head of worldwide procurement and in 2004 he was named vice president of Operations. In 2007, Jeff played a significant role in Apple's entry into the mobile phone market with the launch of the iPhone, and he has led worldwide operations for iPod and iPhone since that time. Prior to Apple, Jeff worked for the IBM Corporation from 1985 to 1998 in a number of operations and engineering roles. He holds a bachelor's degree in Mechanical Engineering from North Carolina State University and an MBA from Duke University.

Scott Forstall
Senior Vice President, iPhone Software
Since: 2008
Compensation: 10,004,755 USD

Mr. Forstall has been the Senior Vice President of iPhone Software at Apple since 2008. He joined Apple in 1997 and is one of the original architects of Mac OS X and its Aqua user interface. Prior to Apple, Mr. Forstall worked at NeXT developing core technologies. He received both Bachelor of Science in Symbolic Systems and Master of Science in Computer Science from Stanford University.

Jonathan Ive
Senior Vice President, Industrial Design

Apple Inc

Mr. Ive is the Senior Vice President of Industrial Design at Apple. Since 1996, he has been responsible for leading the design. Mr. Ive holds a Bachelor of Arts and an honorary Doctorate from Newcastle Polytechnic.

Ronald B. Johnson
Senior Vice President, Retail
Since: 2008

Mr. Johnson has been the Senior Vice President, Retail at Apple since 2008. He joined the company in 2000. Prior to joining the company, Mr. Johnson spent 16 years with Target Stores, most recently serving as the Senior Merchandising Executive.

Robert Mansfield
Senior Vice President, Mac Hardware Engineering
Since: 2008
Compensation: 13,996,589 USD

Mr. Mansfield has been the Senior Vice President of Macintosh Hardware Engineering at Apple since 2008. Prior to joining Apple in 1999, he was the Vice President of Engineering at Raycer Graphics, which Apple acquired in 1999. Previously, Mr. Mansfield was a Senior Director at SGI, responsible for the development of various microprocessor designs. He holds a BSEE degree from The University of Texas at Austin in 1983

Peter Oppenheimer
Senior Vice President and Chief Financial Officer
Compensation: 10,269,720 USD

Mr. Oppenheimer is the Senior Vice President and Chief Financial Officer at Apple. He joined the company in 1996. Mr. Oppenheimer also served with the company in the position of Vice President and Corporate Controller, and as the Senior Director of Finance for the

Americas. Prior to joining the company, he was the Chief Financial Officer of one of the four business units at Automatic Data Processing. Prior to joining ADP, Mr. Oppenheimer spent six years in the information technology consulting practice at Coopers and Lybrand.

Philip W. Schiller
Senior Vice President, Worldwide Product Marketing

Mr. Schiller is the Senior Vice President, Worldwide Product Marketing at Apple. Prior to rejoining Apple in 1997, he was the Vice President of Product Marketing at Macromedia from 1995 to 1997, and a Director of Product Marketing at FirePower Systems from 1993 to 1995. Prior to that, Mr. Schiller spent six years at the company in various marketing positions.

Bertrand Serlet
Senior Vice President, Software Engineering

Mr. Serlet is the Senior Vice President, Software Engineering at Apple. He joined the company in 1997 upon the company's acquisition of NeXT. At NeXT, Mr. Serlet held several engineering and managerial positions, including Director of Web Engineering. Prior to NeXT, he worked as a Research Engineer at Xerox PARC from 1985 to 1989.

D. Bruce Sewell
Senior Vice President, General Counsel and Secretary
Since: 2009

Mr. Sewell has been the Senior Vice President, General Counsel and Secretary at Apple since September 2009. He joined Apple from Intel, where he was responsible for leading all of Intel's legal, corporate affairs and corporate social responsibility programs, managing attorneys and policy professionals located in over 30 countries around the world. Mr. Sewell joined Intel in 1995 as a Senior Attorney assigned to counsel various business groups in areas such as antitrust compliance, licensing and intellectual property. In 2001, he was promoted to Vice President and Deputy General Counsel, managing Intel's litigation portfolio, and handled corporate transactions including M&A activities. Prior to joining Intel, Mr. Sewell was a Partner in the litigation firm of Brown & Bain P.C. He was admitted to the California Bar in 1986 and to the Washington D.C. Bar in 1987. Mr. Sewell is also admitted to practice before the United States Court of Appeals for the Federal Circuit. He received his J.D. from George Washington University in 1986, and a Bachelor of Science degree from the University of Lancaster, in the UK, in 1979.

Board of Directors

William V. Campbell
Director, Non Executive Board
Since: 1997
Compensation: 981,099 USD

Mr. Campbell has been a Director at Apple since 1997. He also has been the Chairman at Intuit since 1998, and a Director since 1994. From 1999 to 2000, Mr. Campbell acted as CEO at Intuit. From 1994 to 1998, he was the President and CEO at Intuit. From 1991 to 1993, Mr. Campbell served as the President and CEO at GO Corporation. He is also the Chair of the Board of Trustees of Columbia University and a Director of the National Football Foundation & College Hall of Fame.

Millard S. Drexler
Director, Non Executive Board
Since: 1999
Compensation: 766,339 USD

Mr. Drexler has been a Director at Apple since 1999. He also has been the Chairman and CEO at J. Crew Group since 2003. Previously, Mr. Drexler was the CEO at Gap from 1995 and President from 1987 to 2002. He was also a Director of Gap from 1983 to 2002.

Albert Gore
Director, Non Executive Board
Since: 2003
Compensation: 436,372 USD

Mr. Gore has been a Director at Apple since 2003. He also has been a Senior Advisor to Google since 2001. Mr. Gore has also been the Chairman at Current TV since 2002, Chairman at Generation Investment Management since 2004 and a Partner at Kleiner Perkins Caufield & Byers since 2007. Mr. Gore is also the Chairman at the Alliance for Climate Protection. He is a visiting professor at the University of California Los Angeles, Fisk University and Middle Tennessee State University. Mr. Gore was inaugurated as the 45th Vice President of the US in 1993. He was re-elected in 1996 and served for a total of eight years as the President of the Senate, a member of the Cabinet and the National Security Council. Prior to 1993, Mr. Gore served for eight years in the US Senate and eight years in the US House of Representatives.

Andrea Jung
Director, Non Executive Board
Since: 2008
Compensation: 707,058 USD

Ms. Jung has been a Director at Apple since 2008. She has also been the Chairman and CEO at Avon Products since 2001. Ms. Jung has been the CEO at Avon since 1999, Chairman since 2001 and Director at the company since 1988. She served as the President at the company from 1998 to 2001, and as the Chief Operating Officer from 1998 to 1999. Ms. Jung joined Avon in 1994 as the President, Product Marketing for Avon US. Previously, she was Executive Vice President at Neiman Marcus from 1991 to 1993 and as Senior Vice President at I. Magnin from 1987 to 1991. Ms. Jung is also a Director at the General Electric, and a member of the N.Y. Presbyterian Hospital Board of Trustees and a Director of Catalyst.

Arthur D. Levinson
Director, Non Executive Board
Since: 2000
Compensation: 994,602 USD

Mr. Levinson has been a Director at Apple since 2000. He also has been the Chairman at Genentech since 1999, and served as its CEO. Mr. Levinson joined Genentech in 1980 and served in a number of executive positions, including Senior Vice President of R&D from 1993 to 1995. He was also a Director at Google.
("Datamonitor, *Apple, Inc.*")

2. Corporate Governance

a. Board Member Responsibilities

"The fundamental role of the directors is to exercise their business judgment to act in what they reasonably believe to be the best interests of the Corporation and its shareholders. In fulfilling that responsibility, directors reasonably may rely on the honesty and integrity of the corporation's senior management and expert legal, accounting, financial and other advisors.

Annual Meeting Attendance
All directors are expected to attend the Corporation's annual meeting of shareholders.

Scheduling of Board Meetings and Attendance
The Board will meet at least four times per year. Directors are expected to prepare for, attend and participate in all Board and applicable committee meetings, and to spend the time needed to meet as often as necessary to discharge their obligations properly.

Agenda
At the beginning of each year the Board will set, to the extent foreseeable and practicable, a schedule of agenda items to be discussed during the year. Any director may suggest items to be included on the agenda or raise subjects at a Board meeting that are not on the agenda for that meeting. An agenda for each Board meeting, along with information and data that is important to the Board's understanding of the business to be conducted at the Board meeting, should be distributed to directors in advance of the meeting, so that Board meeting time may be focused on questions that the Board has about the materials. Certain

matters may be discussed at the meeting without advance distribution of written materials, as appropriate."
("Apple, Inc. Corporate Governance Guidelines", Pages 3-4)

b. Board Committees

The Board currently has a Nominating and Corporate Governance Committee, an Audit and Finance Committee and a Compensation Committee. From time to time, the Board may form new committees as it deems appropriate. The members of the committees are identified in the table below.

Director	Audit Committee	Compensation Committee	Nominating Committee
William V. Campbell	Co-Chair	--	--
Millard S. Drexler	--	Member	Member
Albert A. Gore	--	Member	Member
Steven P. Jobs	--	--	--
Andrea Jung	Member	Chair	--
Arthur D. Levinson, Ph. D.	Co-Chair	--	Chair

Independence and Qualifications of Standing Committee Members
"All of the members of the standing committees will meet the then-effective criteria for independence established by NASDAQ and, in the case of the Audit and Finance Committee, the Sarbanes-Oxley Act of 2002 and the independence definition as set forth in Rule 10A-3(b)(1) of the Securities Exchange Act of 1934, as amended. The members of these committees also will meet the other membership criteria specified in the respective charters for these committees. At least one member of the Compensation Committee will not serve simultaneously on the Audit and Finance Committee."
("Apple, Inc. Corporate Governance Guidelines", Page 4)

Apple Inc

Standing Committee Member Assignments and Rotation

"The Nominating and Corporate Governance Committee makes recommendations to the Board concerning the structure and composition of the Board committees. The Board will designate the chair, committee members and, where applicable, alternate standing committee members, by the vote of a majority of the directors. From time to time, there will be occasions on which the Board may want to rotate standing committee members, but the Board does not believe that it should establish a formal policy of rotation."
("Apple, Inc. Corporate Governance Guidelines", Pages 4-5)

Standing Committee Charters

"Each standing committee will have its own charter. The charter will set forth the purpose, authority and responsibilities of the standing committee in addition to the qualifications for standing committee membership. "
("Apple, Inc. Corporate Governance Guidelines", Page 5)

Meeting and Agenda

"The chair of each standing committee will determine, in consultation with the appropriate standing committee members and members of management, and in accordance with the standing committee's charter, the frequency and length of standing committee meetings and the standing committee's agenda. Each standing committee will establish, to the extent foreseeable and practical, a schedule of agenda items to be discussed during the year. The schedule for each standing committee will be furnished to the full Board."
("Apple, Inc. Corporate Governance Guidelines", Page 5)

Current Committees

Apple currently has three committees: the Audit and Finance Committee, the Compensation Committee, and the Nominating Committee.

Audit Committee

The purpose of this committee is to assist the board in oversight and monitoring of:
1. The corporation's financial statements and other financial information.
2. Compliance with legal, regulatory, and public disclosure requirements.
3. Enterprise risk management; the independent auditors, including their qualifications and independence.
4. The corporation's systems of internal controls.
5. The auditing, accounting, and financial reporting process generally.

This committee shall also prepare the report required by the rules of the Securities and

Exchange Commission (SEC) to be includes in the corporation's annual proxy statement.

Compensation Committee
"The purpose of this committee is to:
1. Establish and modify compensation and incentive plan programs.
2. Review and approve compensation and awards under compensation and incentive plans and programs for elected officers of the corporation.
3. Act as the administering committee for equity compensation plans as designated by the board."

("Apple, Inc. Compensation Committee Charter", Page 1)

Nominating Committee
The purpose of this committee is to:
1. Consider and report periodically to the board on matters relating to the identification, selection, and qualification of board members and candidates nominated to the board.
2. Advise and make recommendations to the board of directors with respect to corporate governance matters.

("Apple, Inc. Nominating and Corporate Governance Committee Charter", Page 1)

c. Director Compensation
"The Compensation Committee will review the form and amount of director compensation annually and recommend any changes to the Board. Non-employee directors are expected to receive a substantial portion of their annual retainer in the form of equity. Employee directors are not paid additional compensation for their services as directors."

("Apple, Inc. Corporate Governance Guidelines", Page 5)

F. Generic Industry Type

i. Domestic

a. 33411 Computer Manufacturing

Industry Definition	Companies in this industry manufacture and/or assemble personal computers, mainframes, workstations, laptops and computer servers. Industry participants may also manufacture computer storage devices that allow the storage and retrieval of data from a phase change, magnetic, optical or magnetic/optical media.
Market Size & growth rate	Revenue : $56.0 billion Profit: $7.8 billion Annual growth (05-10): -5.1% Annual growth (10-15): -0.3% Exports: $43.2 billion Businesses: 1100
Key rivals & market share	Dell Inc: 18.0 % Hewlett-Packard Company 10.0% International Business Machines Corp.: 10% EMC: 5%
Scope of Competitive rivalry	The Industry structure is as follow: Life Cycle Stage is Declining, Revenue Volatility is Medium, Investment Requirements is Low, Industry Assistance is Low, Concentration Level is medium, Regulation Level is Light, Technology Change is High, Barriers to Entry is high, Industry Globalization is High, and Competition Level is High. The Leader of the Industry is Dell at 18.0%. The other top three are Hewlett-Packard Company, International Business Machines Corporation, and EMC Corporation.

Apple Inc

Concentration vs. fragmentation	Given that the four largest firms (Dell, HP, IBM, and EMC) account for 43% of the overall market-share, this industry is considered fragmented and highly competitive.

The Herfindahl-Hirschman Index supports the fact that the industry is fragmented, thus highly competitive. |
| Number of buyers | Key Buying Industries:

42142 Copy Machine and Office Supplies Wholesaling in the US

42143 Computer, Peripheral and Packages Software Wholesaling in the US

44-45 Retail Trade in the US

44312 Computer Stores in the US

52 Finance and Insurance in the US

92 Public Administration in the US

The major end-market segments for computers and computer peripherals include wholesalers and retailers, as well as direct sales to end-markets. End-consumer markets include households, business and government.

In 2010, the total market-cap for the Computer & Peripheral Manufacturing Industry was $54.6 billion dollars. |
| Demand Determinants | Price of computers and peripheral equipment: Declining real prices for computers and associated peripherals can adversely affect profit margins and focus attention on costs structures. On the other hand, declining prices for these products can drive an increase in demand for these products.

Per capita disposable income affects consumer spending on computer and peripheral equipment. |

Apple Inc

| | Trade-weighted index: Foreign exchange rate movements affect the competitiveness of US manufactured products (both against imports and export markets).

Exchange rate movements can increase or decrease the US dollar price of imports coming into the United States and can increase or decrease the foreign currency price of US exports (i.e. in the currency of a particular export market).

Private investment in computers and software: General levels of economic activity and resulting levels of economy-wide investment spending influence expenditure on industry products. Businesses tend to cut capital when economic conditions are adverse.

Gross Domestic Product (GDP): The level of economic activity influences business and household demand for computers and peripheral products. Growth in investment by the service sector of the economy on computers and computer peripherals has been relatively higher compared with other sectors of the economy, partly reflecting strong growth in the services sector of the US economy. |
|---|---|
| Degree of product Differentiation | The industry demonstrates a low degree of differentiation, as software (specifically operating systems) mostly accounts for product distinction. |
| Product Innovation | Companies in this industry rely more so on innovating new products more so than any other industry. |
| Key Success Factors | Establishing a brand name, Intensive research and development and the development of the new products, appropriate product pricing, building a product range. |
| Supply/demand conditions | Impacted by the economy. When economy was strong in 2006 & 2007 sales and demand were also strong. As economy has struggled the supply/demand conditions have become less. |
| Analysis of Stage in life cycle | Product life cycles are short, and new product introductions are regular. The industry life cycle as a whole is in decline. |
| Pace of Technological | Technological change in this industry is rapid. |

Apple Inc

change	
Vertical Integration	Vertical integration is achieved through means of direct marketing or retailing outlets.
Economies of Scale	Growths in production volumes tend to increase the economies of scale. The fall in computer prices is attributed partly by a rise in economies of scale. Major companies also tend to outsource to manufacturers who specialize in production and supply chain processes.
Learning/experience curve effects	Research and development is high in this industry. R&D is conducted to protect existing customer and product bases and to generate growth opportunities. Major players in this industry tend to spend a large percentage on R&D to provide them with innovations to be able to move into low-price markets. Outsourcing production and supply chains will not slow down in this industry. Companies will continue this to help drive unit cost down.
Barriers to entry	This industry is believed to have high barriers to entry. Major barriers include high levels of capital, research and development (R&D) investments and large-scale operations. Barriers to entry checklist level Competition High Concentration Medium Life cycle stage Decline Investment requirements Low Technology change High Regulation and policy Light Industry assistance Low
Regulation/ Deregulation	Manufacturers in this industry can be subject to regulation by various federal and state governmental agencies. Such regulation includes the radio frequency emission regulatory activities of the Federal Communications Commission, the anti-trust regulatory activities of the Federal Trade Commission and Department of Justice, the import/export regulatory activities of the Department of Commerce and the product safety regulatory activities of the Consumer Products Safety Commission.

Globalization	This industry has a high level of globalization. For 2010, exports are forecast to represent 77.2% of industry revenue; and imports are forecast to represent 86.3% of domestic demand.
Trends	The introduction of new peripheral products spurred large growth in industry establishments. There has been a shift toward mobile computing; however, growth in unit sales was moderated by an ongoing decline in average selling prices.

b. 33422 Communication Equipment Manufacturing

Industry Definition	This industry includes firms engaged in manufacturing radio and television broadcast and wireless communications equipment. Examples of products made by these firms are: transmitting and receiving antennas, cable television equipment, GPS equipment, pagers, cellular phones, mobile communications equipment, and radio and television studio and broadcasting equipment.
Market Size & growth rate	Revenue: $38.7bn Profit: $3.6bn Annual Growth Rate 05-10: -0.5% Annual Growth Rate 10-15: .03%. Exports: $4.7bn Businesses: 917
Key rivals & market share	Motorola, Inc.: 30.0% Harris Corporation: 9.5% Alcatel-Lucent: 4.5%
Scope of Competitive rivalry	The Industry structure is as follow: Life Cycle Stage is Declining, Revenue Volatility is High, Investment Requirements is High, Industry Assistance is Low, Concentration Level is medium, Regulation Level is Heavy, Technology Change is High, Barriers to Entry is high, Industry Globalization is High, and Competition Level is High. There are three major players in this industry. Motorola, Inc is the

	clear leader at 30% and the nearest competitor is Harris Corporation at 9.5%.
Concentration vs. Fragmentation	Given that the three largest firms (Motorola, Harris, and Alcatel-Lucent) account for 44% of the overall market-share, this industry is considered fragmented and highly competitive. The Herfindahl-Hirschman Index supports the fact that the industry is fragmented, thus highly competitive.
Number of Buyers	Key Buying Industries Radio Broadcasting in the US Radio broadcasting equipment is sold to companies in this industry. Television Broadcasting in the US TV broadcasting equipment is required by companies in this industry. Cable Networks in the US Cable networks purchase TV broadcasting equipment from communication equipment manufacturers. Wireless Telecommunications Carriers in the US Carrier equipment is required by firms in this industry. 50% Communication service operators, 25% Radio and TV broadcasters, and 25% Installers, retailers and wholesalers
Demand Determinants	Downstream demand from wireless telecommunications carriers The cost and breadth of wireless telecommunication services in the United States, and globally, affects the demand for these services and for enabling equipment. Gross domestic product (GDP) Economic growth impacts capital and consumption spending on industry products, and therefore has a positive effect on this industry. Trade-weighted index Local manufacturers compete with imports in local markets and therefore the level of the US dollar exchange rate

Apple Inc

	relative to overseas competitors can be an important influence on profit margins and sales. Similarly, local manufacturers compete with overseas-based firms in export markets and movements in the US dollar relative to the currency of competitors can also be important. Downstream demand from television broadcasting The cost and breadth of TV services in the United States and globally affects the demand for these services and for enabling equipment. Downstream demand from radio broadcasting The cost and breadth of radio services in the United States and globally affects the demand for these services and for enabling equipment.
Degree of product Differentiation	As evidenced by the segmentation within this industry, a low degree of differentiation exists. The breakdown is 46%Radio station equipment, 31%Other communication systems and equipment, 13%Wireless networking equipment, and 10%Broadcast, studio, and related electronic equipment.
Product Innovation	Technological innovation characterizes this industry more than most others. Innovations, along with increasing demands from consumers for services and devices that facilitate mobility, are major factors that have driven demand for communication equipment.
Key Success Factors	Effective quality control, production of a range which accommodates future developments, having technology sharing arrangements with major players, having contacts within key markets, superior financial & debt management, ability to compete on tender, effective cost controls, undertaking technical research and development, ability to quickly adopt new technology, having marketing expertise.
Supply/demand conditions	Capital spending decisions by wireless communications service providers will be affected by the following: growth in the number of wireless subscribers; growth in network traffic; network capacity utilization; network operating costs; expectations of demand for new wireless services; the development of technologies and standards; and competitive factors.
Analysis of Stage in	Technology is progressing rapidly, which is creating opportunities for

life cycle	the industry to supply new products. Standards and regulations are also accommodating and promoting new markets. Production is being transferred to low labor-cost countries. Globally, the industry is in a long-term growth phase, however, in the United States it is in decline.
Pace of Technological change	The pace of technological change in this industry is high.
Vertical Integration	Firms in this industry can develop all components of the device. They can manufacture the integrated circuits and also develop the software to drive the handsets. Production can be outsourced to specialist contract electronics manufacturers, however, these same low-cost firms can turn around and begin developing their own products.
Economies of Scale	Economies of scale are achieved through acquisitions of competitors, lowering labor costs, and close proximity to raw materials and other electronic manufacturers.
Learning/experience curve effects	Larger companies will have an advantage over smaller companies due to the enormous amount of research and development. Mergers of companies that have different communications protocols, i.e. CDMA and LTE, are expected to lower unit cost.
Barriers to entry	Barriers to entry in this industry are considered to be high overall due mainly to the following: the high technological base of the industry, which can require significant investment in research and development in order to produce attractive proprietary products; the costs involved in developing a reputation and a brand name; and the costs involved in attracting skilled employees.
Regulation/ Deregulation	The Federal Communications Commission (FCC) is an independent United States government agency, directly responsible to Congress. The FCC was established by the Communications Act of 1934 and is charged with regulating interstate and international communications by radio, television, wire, satellite and cable. The allocation of radio frequencies affects the introduction of new wireless technologies. FCC type acceptance regulations require that products meet specified radio frequency emission standards and not cause unallowable

 Apple Inc

	interference with other services.
Globalization	There is a high level of globalization in this industry. Foreign-owned companies are currently estimated to account for over 30% of the value of industry shipments. Imports for Consumption are expected to account for 55.8% of the value of domestic demand in 2010 (with some of these imports coming from subsidiaries of US companies or from overseas-based contract manufacturers), while US Domestic Exports are expected to account for 12.4% of industry shipments in the same year.
Trends	The value of industry shipments declined at an average annualized real rate of 6.6% in the five years through 2005, (although the rate of change was volatile from year-to-year). This followed a very strong period of growth in industry shipments between 1992 and 2000 (growing at an average annualized real rate of 9.8%). In 2000, the real value of industry shipments surged 26.0%, despite an increase in import penetration, due to massive real growth in domestic demand (up 40.7%). Growth in domestic demand for industry products between 1998 and 2000 was mainly the result of a growing market for mobile wireless equipment, with mobile communications service providers rapidly building networks in response to demand. The original networks were built using first-generation (1G) analog technology. In the early 1990s, wireless communications networks advanced from analog to digital technology based systems, including TDMA, CDMA, and GSM, and this brought forward significant investment in new equipment.

c. 33411a Portables IPOD Industry

Industry Definition	Companies in this industry manufacture, design or assemble personal computers (PCs), laptops, handheld computers and servers. Industry operators typically purchase computer components (e.g. graphics cards and motherboards) from dedicated manufacturers in other industries (see report 33441a – Semiconductor & Circuit Manufacturing). Manufacturers of computer monitors, mice, keyboards and printers are covered in 33411b – Computer Monitor

Apple Inc

	and Peripheral Manufacturing.
Market Size & growth rate	Revenue: $48.0bn Profit: $1.7bn Annual Growth 05-10: 0.9% Annual Growth 10-15: -7% Exports: $6.9bn Businesses: 435
Key rivals & market share	Hewlett-Packard Company: 27.3% Dell Inc.: 26.3% International Business Machines Corporation: 14.9% Apple Computer Inc.: 8.5%
Scope of Competitive rivalry	The Industry structure is as follow: Life Cycle Stage is Declining, Revenue Volatility is Medium, Investment Requirements is Low, Industry Assistance is Low, Concentration Level is High, Regulation Level is Light, Technology Change is High, Barriers to Entry is Low, Industry Globalization is High, and Competition Level is High. There are two big players which are Hewlett Packard Company and Dell Inc. They each have 26% of the market but Hewlett Packard is the leader with 27.3%. The other big players are International Business Machines Corporation and Apple Computer Inc rounds out the top four with 8.5%.
Concentration vs. Fragmentation	Portables Manufacturing Market Concentration breakdown as Dell 26.3%, HP 27.3%, IBM 14.9%, Apple 8.5%, and other 23%. Given that the four largest firms (HP, Dell, IBM, and Apple) account for 77% of the overall market-share, this industry is considered highly concentrated. In Herfindahl-Hirschman Index Portables HP have 745.92, Dell 691.69, IBM 222.01, Apple 72.25, and other 529 in 2010 The Herfindahl-Hirschman Index supports the fact that the industry is concentrated.
Number of Buyers	Key Buying Industries

Apple Inc

	Information in the US Information services businesses purchases computers and servers to efficiently deliver information to customers. Public Administration in the US Government agencies buys computers primarily for use by public employees. Consumers in the US Consumers buy computers for personal use, including entertainment and internet access.
Demand Determinants	Domestic price of personal computers Computer manufacturers experience lower revenue as retail computer prices fall. These declining prices are largely the result of more productive manufacturing methods and competition from abroad. As these prices continue to fall, computer manufacturing will become increasingly commoditized. Consumer sentiment index Consumer confidence plays an important role in the purchases of durable goods. When consumers are particularly confident, they are most likely to purchase durable goods like computers, appliances and vehicles. Corporate profits Corporations are a major customer base for computer manufacturers, particularly for high-end equipment like servers and workstations. Companies need to replace their computers periodically, because of the rapid rate of technological change in this industry, but their purchase timing can be significantly affected by the level of corporate profits. When companies are losing money or otherwise struggling to survive, they tend to delay making investments in their computing infrastructure. Downstream demand from data processing services Data processing service providers and data centers in general are major purchasers of computers, particularly servers. When these industries expand they purchase more computers. Trade-weighted index Increases in the trade-weighted value of the US dollar inflate the cost of purchasing US-made computers, causing customers to switch to relatively less expensive products produced elsewhere.

Degree of product Differentiation	As evidenced by the segmentation within this industry, a low degree of differentiation exists.
Product Innovation	Tablet computers hold great promise, offering intuitive touch-screen access to the internet, videos, music, books and games in a form factor that is comfortable and portable.
Key Success Factors	Ability to quickly adopt new technology, effective advertising and branding, effective cost controls, strength in export markets, offering a "one-stop shop"
Supply/demand conditions	Demand for new computers is primarily driven by technological advancements by semiconductor manufacturers, computer prices, corporate profits and consumer sentiment. However, while falling computer prices boost computer sales, they also drive larger shares of computer demand into the hands of foreign computer manufacturers, who benefit from lower production costs.
Analysis of Stage in life cycle	Computers are trending toward commoditization. Industry activity is increasingly concentrated within a few firms. International competitors increasingly dominate this industry. Overall the industry is in decline.
Pace of Technological change	The pace of technological change in this industry is high.
Vertical Integration	Vertical integration is achieved through means of direct marketing or retailing outlets.
Economies of Scale	Most competitors in this industry are involved in manufacturing and assembly and distribution but few are also involved in retailing of their product. Most sell their product to outside retailers and few have their own retail outlets. Falling prices for computers means less profit. To increase the profit margin, and further reduce costs, manufacturers are diverting more production overseas.
Learning/experience curve effects	Unit costs have decreased as semi-conductor prices have decreased. Most components come to these manufacturers as finished sub-assemblies. These sub-assemblies are relatively simple to assemble which keeps labor requirements fairly low, further driving costs down.

Barriers to entry	The Computer Manufacturing industry has very low barriers to entry, with no signs of increasing in the near future. On a small scale, computer assembly is a simple task due to the highly standardized nature of computer components. Computer component manufacturers build their products according to set industry standards, allowing for a wide degree of compatibility with components from other manufacturers. Assembling computers is as simple as snapping in purchased components into appropriate slots within computer cases, which are also provided by suppliers. Many computer manufacturers, including Dell and Apple, began with the company's founders assembling machines in their garages. The extreme ease of entry makes this industry exceptionally price-competitive.
Regulation/ Deregulation	Computer manufacturers face minimal regulatory intervention in practice. However, several regulatory bodies have nominal oversight over industry activities. As with other electronics manufacturers, computer manufacturers must comply with radio frequency emissions standards put forth by the US Federal Communications Commission (FCC), certifying that computers do not emit a problematic level of radio waves which may interfere with other broadcasts. Along with most other businesses, computer manufacturers face antitrust regulations from the Federal Trade Commission (FTC) and the Department of Justice (DoJ). Product safety requirements are enforced by the US Consumer Product Safety Commission. The regulatory activities of these bodies rarely have significant effects on the operations of computer manufacturers, as the relevant regulations rarely change.
Globalization	The Computer Manufacturing industry is highly affected by globalization. Computer imports represent 79.5% of domestic demand. Industry supply chains are highly complex, with virtually every manufacturer assembling computers from imported semiconductors and computer chips. The largest companies in this industry operate on a global scale, with manufacturing facilities on multiple continents. Currently, foreign ownership of US producers is fairly low. In 2007, Acer, a major Taiwanese computer manufacturer, bought US-based Gateway Inc. for $710 million. This was the last major foreign acquisition of a US-based computer manufacturer,

	though Acer has since moved all production to Asia and is retaining Gateway principally for its brand name.
Trends	Census data indicates that industry revenue decreased at an average annualized real rate of 1.7% in the 13 years through 2005, with real growth in revenue in the five years through 1997 offset by a real decrease in revenue in the eight years through 2005 (there were real declines in revenue in six of the eight years, including a 21.3% real decline in 2001 and an 18.2% real decline in 2002). The real decline in revenue in the eight years through 2005 mainly resulted from rapidly falling unit selling prices, a significant increase in import penetration and slow or negative real growth in industry exports.

ii. Global

a. Global Computer & Peripherals

Industry Definition	The global computers and peripherals industry comprises of the global computer hardware market and the global computer storage & peripherals market. Any currency conversions used in the creation of this report have been calculated using constant annual average exchange rates. The computer hardware market consists of personal computers, servers, mainframes, workstations, and peripherals. The market value figure relates to end-user spending on hardware. Market segmentations relate to spending on personal computers and other computer hardware (including mainframes, servers, and peripherals). The computer storage and peripherals market includes manufacturers of electronic computer components and peripherals, such as data storage components, motherboards, audio and video cards, monitors, keyboards, printers and other peripherals. The market value excludes semiconductors classified in the Semiconductors sub-industry. The market value relates to end-user spending on storage and peripherals.
Market Size & growth rate	Market Value:

	The global computers and peripherals industry grew by 5.1% in 2008 to reach a value of $540.1 billion. Market Value Forecast: In 2013, the global computers and peripherals industry is forecast to have a value of $720 billion, an increase of 33.3% since 2008.
Key rivals & market share	Hewlett-Packard Company 16.90% International Business Machines Corporation 10.80% Dell Computer Corporation 10.10% Toshiba Corporation 8.40% Other 53.80%
Scope of Competitive rivalry	The computer and peripherals industry is dominated by a number of large players such as Hewlett-Packard and Dell. The concentration of the industry is a continuing trend, with merger and acquisition activity being common. There are significant pricing pressures within the industry that act to intensify rivalry between players. However, a number of companies attempt to offset such pressures by outsourcing the manufacturing of certain computer components to contract manufacturers in Asia-Pacific. Rapidly improving technology in both size and functionality, combined with the demands of new software upon platform requirements, leads to relatively short product-lifecycles for PC hardware. Although bolstering overall computer sales, this places significant demands upon manufacturers to keep up with rapidly changing consumer trends, whilst generating a fiercely competitive environment. A number of larger players within this industry are large conglomerates (e.g. IBM and Toshiba). Such companies have highly diversified operations, which alleviates rivalry to an extent. Overall, rivalry within this industry is assessed as moderate.
Concentration vs. fragmentation	The Top 5 Companies own 46.2%, this industry is considered concentrated Hewlett-Packard Company 16.90%

Apple Inc

	International Business Machines Corporation 10.80% Dell Computer Corporation 10.10% Toshiba Corporation 8.40% Other 53.80%
Number of buyers	Major buyers of products in this industry are business customers for whose operations such equipment is often indispensable. Business customers often have supply contracts with individual manufacturers and therefore often incur significant switching costs.
Demand Determinants	Brand image can play an important role in this industry, with companies such as Hewlett-Packard relying upon their strong brand image to maximize sales. However, although brand awareness is high, customers are generally more interested in the quality and specifications of individual products, and customer loyalty is therefore relatively low. Buyer power within this industry is assessed as moderate overall.
Degree of product Differentiation	PCs 43.90% Server and Networking 26.50% Printers 9.40% Data Storage 9.30% Monitors 7.20% Other 3.70% Personal computers (PC) segment accounts for 43.9% of the global computers and peripherals industry's value. Europe 37.20% Americas 36.30% Asia-Pacific 21.40% Rest of the World 5.00% Europe accounts for 37.2% of the global computers and peripherals industry's value.
Product Innovation	Product innovation is the key in order to be successful in the industry. R&D is key in order to bring new and improved products to the market

Key Success Factors	Continuous R & D, Brand awareness, outsourcing costs to keep prices low
Supply/demand conditions	Supplies for this industry have minimal differentiation and are often outsourced to keep costs low
Analysis of Stage in life cycle	Industry is in a decline but is slowly expected to rise by 2013
Pace of Technological change	The pace of technological change in this industry is high.
Vertical Integration	Companies can be backward integrated by manufacturing components and then using them in their own product. Forwards vertical integration can occur by the manufacturer owning and operating their own retail outlets.
Economies of Scale	Economies of scale in this industry can be achieved through better bargaining power with supplier, better global marketing and distribution networks, bigger research and development budgets, a greater ability to shift productions costs and tax liabilities to the most advantageous countries, and by attracting top managerial talent.
Learning/experience curve effects	Companies in this industry have gone to outside contractors to manufacture certain computer components and assemblies to drive down the cost per unit.
Barriers to entry	Major buyers of products in this industry are business customers for whose operations such equipment is often indispensable. Business customers often have supply contracts with individual manufacturers and therefore often incur significant switching costs. Suppliers to the computer and peripherals industry generally include electronic component manufacturers. The majority of components supplied to this industry display minimal differentiation and, in order to reduce costs, are often sourced from companies operating from low-cost manufacturing regions. Manufacturers do not incur significant costs when switching basic component suppliers and, in such instances, supplier power is low.
Regulation/ Deregulation	Protection of intellectual property by defending patents is an additional cost for manufacturers. Companies rely on patent,

Apple Inc

	copyright, trademark and trade secret laws and contract rights to establish and maintain proprietary rights in technology and products. Regulation/Deregulation also varies from country to country.
Globalization	The global computers and peripherals industry grew by 5.1% in 2008 to reach a value of $540.1 billion. In 2013, the global computers and peripherals industry is forecast to have a value of $720 billion, an increase of 33.3% since 2008. Personal computers (PC) segment accounts for 43.9% of the global computers and peripherals industry's value. Europe accounts for 37.2% of the global computers and peripherals industry's value. Hewlett-Packard Company accounts for 16.9% of the global computers and peripherals industry's value.
Trends	The performance of the industry is forecast to accelerate only slightly, with an anticipated CAGR of 5.9% for the five-year period 2008-2013. This is expected to drive the industry to a value of $720 billion by the end of 2013. This will be an increase of 33.3% since 2008. The compound annual growth rate of the industry in the period 2008-2013 is predicted to be 5.9%.

b. Global Communication Equipment

Industry Definition	The communications equipment market covers fixed-line and mobile telecommunications equipment. The fixed-line telecommunications equipment includes answer machines, fax machines and telephones. The mobile telecommunications equipment includes mobile phone handsets only and not any services related charges borne by the consumer. The market is valued at retail selling price (RSP) with any currency conversions calculated using constant 2008 annual average exchange rates. For the purpose of this report the global figure is deemed to comprise of the Americas, Asia-Pacific and Europe. The Americas comprises Argentina, Brazil, Canada, Chile, Colombia, Mexico, Venezuela, and the United States. Europe comprises Belgium, the Czech Republic, Denmark, France, Germany, Hungary, Italy, Netherlands, Norway, Poland, Romania, Russia, Spain, Sweden, the Ukraine and the United Kingdom. Asia-Pacific comprises

	Australia, China, Japan, India, Singapore, South Korea and Taiwan.
Market Size & growth rate	Market Value: The global communications equipment market grew by 8.3% in 2008 to reach a value of $51.5 billion. Market Value Forecast: In 2013, the global communications equipment market is forecast to have a value of $71.3 billion, an increase of 38.4% since 2008.
Key rivals & market share	Electricals and Electronics Retailers 66.90% Hypermarket, Supermarket, and Discounters 19.40% Discount, Variety Store, and General Merchandise Retailers 6.90% Cash and Carries and Warehouse Clubs 0.50% Other 6.30%
Scope of Competitive rivalry	Larger players within the industry are multinational players such as Huawei Technologies Co. Ltd., Cisco, LM Ericsson Telephone Company or Motorola, where between whom there is fierce competition despite a high degree of product differentiation. The competition is not only about the biggest market share but it also involves the potential business partners, such as Microsoft. Rivalry is enhanced further by high fixed costs needed for the production process and exits costs created by production facilities. The healthy market growth rate lessens the need to compete for limited revenue and so lowers rivalry. Overall, the level of rivalry within the communications equipment market is moderate.
Concentration vs. fragmentation	The top four companies own the major of the market, this industry is considered concentrated.
Number of buyers	The mobile phone market has reached a high degree of penetration, with a high degree of choice available for consumers. The increasing commoditization of communications equipment indicates an increase in buyer power, although the level of diversification of the equipment is very high. The product specifications vary greatly in technical details, the targeted customers (e.g. military and civil equipment), and the way the data is transferred. All of these detract from buyer power

	as does the huge number of potential buyers, often relatively small in size.
Demand Determinants	The threat of substitutes is almost non-existent as there are not many available current alternatives. However, technology is always advancing and despite these advances coming from within current market players, large companies could diversify into the market with a substitute product.
Degree of product Differentiation	Category Electricals and Electronics Retailers 66.90% Hypermarket, Supermarket, and Discounters 19.40% Discount, Variety Store, and General Merchandise Retailers 6.90% Cash and Carries and Warehouse Clubs 0.50% Other 6.30% Geography Asia-Pacific 51.70% Americas 24.90% Europe 23.40%
Product Innovation	Innovation has progressed over the past few years, especially in the cell phone market. R&D is a big part as the consumers demands has been increasing
Key Success Factors	R & D, Brand Name, Reliable Product
Supply/demand conditions	Manufactures require suppliers to have high end raw material to produce a better quality product
Analysis of Stage in life cycle	The market is beginning to decelerate
Pace of Technological change	The pace of technological change in this industry is high.
Vertical Integration	Vertical integration between electrical component manufacturers is uncommon with the exception of some larger players. Backwards and forwards vertical integration is not very likely especially as the buyers are end users of the equipment.

Economies of Scale	Larger companies in this industry achieve economies of scale due to their substantial research and development resources, international distribution channels, and established relationships with the major telephone companies.
Learning/experience curve effects	Research and development costs are high, which add to the cost per unit. With a high pace of technological change, R&D budgets remain high to create new products.
Barriers to entry	The threat of new entrants into the communications equipment market is moderate. A high level of product differentiation combined with high fixed costs of manufacturing facilities present significant barriers to entry for new players. However, the importance of brand strength within the market is waning especially with respect to networking equipment, with manufacturers shifting from the manufacture of proprietary products to lower priced industry standards. The small end-users switching costs act in favor of new entrants, as does a healthy market growth rate and high consumer demand.
Regulation/ Deregulation	Protection of intellectual property by defending patents is an additional cost for manufacturers. Companies rely on patent, copyright, trademark and trade secret laws and contract rights to establish and maintain proprietary rights in technology and products. Regulation/Deregulation also varies from country to country.
Globalization	The global communications equipment market grew by 8.3% in 2008 to reach a value of $51.5 billion. The compound annual growth rate of the market in the period 2004-2008 was 10.6%. Electricals and electronics retailers dominated the global communications equipment market in 2008, generating 66.9% of the market's overall revenues. Sales made by hypermarket, supermarket, and discounters generated 19.4% of the market's aggregate revenues. Asia-Pacific accounts for 51.7% of the global communications equipment market's value. In comparison, Americas accounts for a further 24.9% of the market's value.
Trends	In 2013, the global communications equipment market is forecast to have a value of $71.3 billion, an increase of 38.4% since 2008. The performance of the market is forecast to decelerate, with an anticipated CAGR of 6.7% for the five-year period 2008-2013, which

Apple Inc

is expected to drive the market to a value of $71.3 billion by the end of 2013. Comparatively, the European and Asia-Pacific markets will grow with CAGRs of 6.9% and 8% respectively, over the same period, to reach respective values of $16.8 billion and $39.2 billion in 2013.

G. Organization structure

this is an organizational outline of the top employees of Apple Inc. They use a typical Functional Organizational Structure where the President is on top and the CEO, CFO, COO follow. Next come the Division Managers. Worldwide Product Marketing, an Advisor, Software Engineer, Design Artist, Applications, and a General Counsel are all part of the Corporate Services division in Apple. Under the Division Mangers come the employees. Above president are the stockholders who elect the Board of Directors.

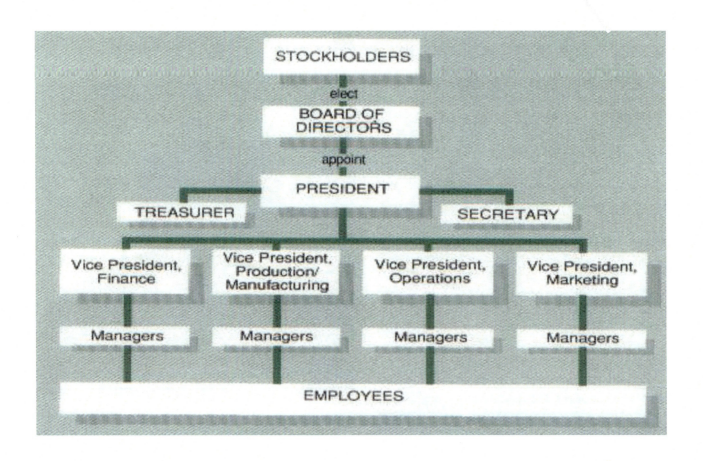

1. **Advantages & Disadvantages**

Advantages to using this method:
- This can assist in structuring a single business.
- This provides a strategically relevant way to organize the business portfolio.
- Promotes a more cohesive and collaborative business.
- Allows strategic planning to be completed.
- Helps allocate corporate resources.

Disadvantages to using this method:
- There can often be a lack of communication between groups.
- Some bad decisions can be made from lower level managers.
- Adds another layer to top management.
- Very little strategy or collaboration is likely to occur.
- Performance recognition gets blurred.

H. Financial Analysis

Apple's diverse product portfolio leads the firm to compete within several separate industries. Given this, we have chosen a representative sample of leaders amongst said industries: Google, RIM, and Dell.

Google's Android device has recently overcome the iPhone as the second most popular wireless operating system (in the US market), Research in Motion owns top market share in the aforementioned wireless segment, and Dell's core business focuses on the production of desktop, laptop, and notebook personal computers whereas

It should be noted that these firms, although similar and often in direct competition, exist in separate industries. Because of the unique demands of each industry, our chosen firms may compare more or less favorably depending upon their core business. For example, Google does not engage in cost-intensive manufacturing and subsequently demonstrates an advantage in cost of goods sold, which greatly affects some profitability ratios.

This section will analyze the financial data generated by these companies, which will be organized into five subsections: overview, profitability, liquidity, leverage, and other.

1. Graphs

Overview

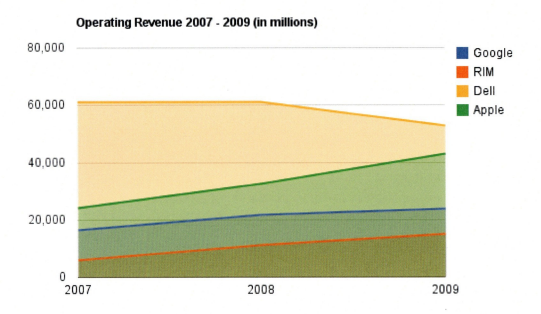

Our first chart examines the operating revenue of our sample of firms from 2007 - 2009 (all subsequent, multi-year charts and graphs will examine the same time period). Simply put, this represents the cash generated through operations and other activities.

Our sample demonstrates the following changes over the period:

Google: +42.52%
RIM: +148.84%
Dell: -4.63%
Apple: +103.72%

In order to gain a greater context, let us compare these results with the following industries:

Industry: Computer Manufacturing in the United States (33411a)
Annual Growth 05-10 years: .9%

Industry: Communications Equipment Manufacturing in the United States (33422)
Annual Growth 05-10 years: -.5%

Industry: Portable Electronics Manufacturing (sic code)
Annual Growth 05-10 years: .9%

The next logical question would be: in light of flat to negative industry growth, what contributed to Apple's substantial revenue increase?

Let us first examine Apple's revenue by Operating Segment and/or geographic region.

Our sample demonstrates the following changes over the period:

Americas: +39.20%
Europe: +71.52%
Japan: +69.31%
Retail: +59.75%
other (includes Asia Pacific and FileMaker): +49.74%

Apple was able to improve performance across all distribution channels, but this only partially reveals the reasons for the organization's success.

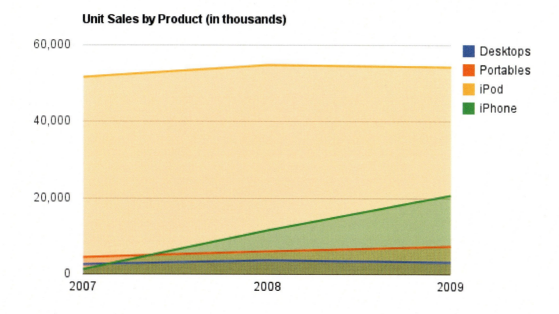

Source: Apple 2009 annual report
Our sample demonstrates the following changes over the period:

Desktops: +17%

Portables (includes iMac, Mac mini, Mac Pro, and Xserve product lines): +66.33%
iPod: +4.8%
iPhone: +1,392.51%

The explosive growth of the iPhone enabled other revenue streams for Apple, as evidenced by the next graph.

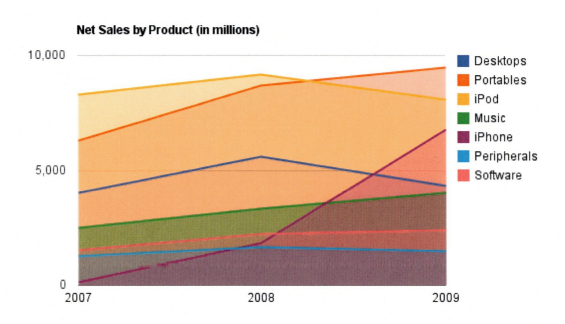

Source: Apple 2009 annual report

Our sample demonstrates the following changes over the period:

Desktops: +7.16%
Portables: +50.49%
iPod: -2.57%
Music (includes iTunes Store sales, iPod services, and Apple branded third-party iPod accessories): +61.70%
iPhone (derived from handset sales, carrier agreements, and Apple branded third-party iPhone accessories): +5,391.05%
Peripherals (includes displays, wireless connectivity and networking solutions, and other hardware accessories): +16.66%
Software: +59.55%

Let us return to our original question: in light of flat to negative industry growth, what contributed to Apple's substantial revenue increase?

Apple's growth in a sagging industry supports the importance of product diversification. Specifically, the introduction of the iPhone and subsequent services generated new and significant revenue streams for the firm.

Liquidity Ratios

The **current ratio** measures whether or not a firm has enough resources to pay its debts over the next 12 months.

For example, if a company's current assets are $50,000 and its current liabilities are $40,000, then its current ratio would be $50,000 divided by $40,000, which equals 1.25. It means that for every dollar the company owes it has $1.25 available in current assets. A current ratio of assets to liabilities of 2:1 is usually considered to be acceptable (current assets are twice your current liabilities).

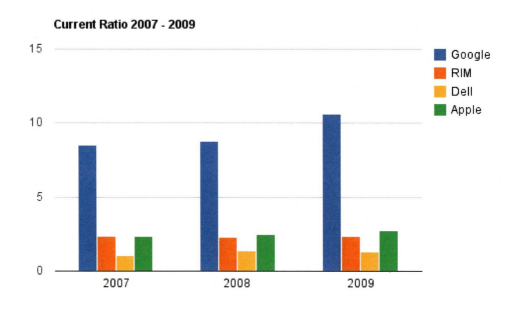

	Google	RIM	Dell	Apple
2007	8.49	2.36	1.07	2.36
2008	8.77	2.29	1.36	2.46
2009	10.62	2.39	1.28	2.74

Apple compares favorably with most firms in this sample yet is dwarfed by Google. Nevertheless, Apple does exceed the acceptable 2-1 standard ratio.

The **quick ratio** (or liquid ratio / acid test) measures the ability of a company to use its quick assets to immediately retire its current liabilities. Quick assets can be quickly converted to cash at close to their book values. A company with a Quick Ratio of less than 1 may struggle to pay back its current liabilities.

The quick ratio is a more conservative measurement than current ratio, as it excludes inventory from current assets.

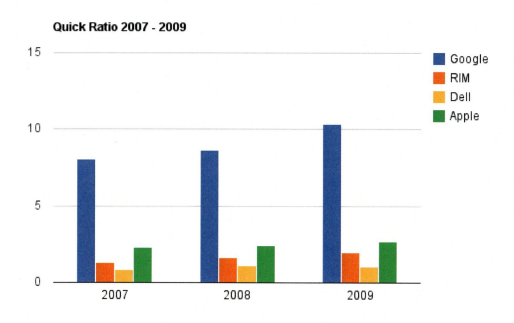

	Google	RIM	Dell	Apple
2007	8.05	1.32	.86	2.09
2008	8.64	1.62	1.09	2.07
2009	10.37	1.94	1.04	2.48

Again, Apple compares favorably with most firms in this sample yet is dwarfed by Google. Nevertheless, Apple does exceed the acceptable 2-1 standard ratio.

Leverage Ratios

The **debt ratio** measures total debt against total assets, and indicates the percentage of a company's assets that are provided via debt. For example, a company with $2 million in total assets and $500,000 in total liabilities would have a debt ratio of 25%

a high ratio is unfavorable and may indicate risk to a firm's on-going operation. Furthermore, a high debt to assets ratio may indicate a low borrowing capacity, thus lowers the organization's financial Flexibility.

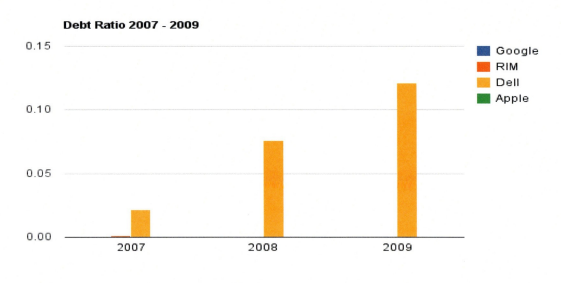

	Google	RIM	Dell	Apple
2007	n/a	.138%	2.13%	n/a
2008	n/a	n/a	7.59%	n/a
2009	n/a	n/a	12.12%	n/a

In light of the aforementioned current and quick ratios, the above table is predictable; against the rest of the sample, Dell has the least capacity to pay-back debt through the immediate liquidation of assets. Thus, Dell is the only firm in our sample significantly leveraging debt (and this use is increasing).

Activity Ratios

The **asset turnover ratio** measures the amount of sales generated for every dollar's worth of assets. It is calculated by dividing sales in dollars by assets in dollars. This measures a firm's efficiency at using its assets to generate revenue; a relatively higher number is desirable. The asset turnover ratio can also indicates pricing strategy: companies with low profit margins tend to have high asset turnover, while those with high profit margins demonstrate the converse.

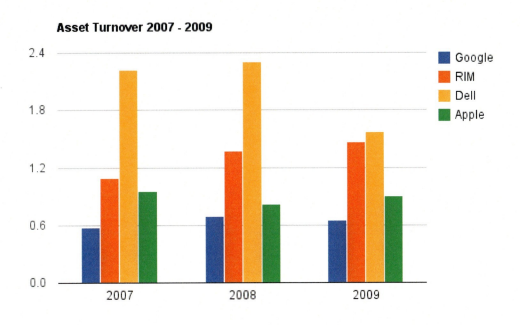

	Google	RIM	Dell	Apple
2007	.65	1.09	2.22	.95
2008	.69	1.37	2.31	.82
2009	.58	1.47	1.57	.90

Inventory turnover is a measure of the number of times inventory is sold or used in any given reporting period.

A low turnover rate may indicate overstocking, obsolescence, or deficiencies in the product line and/ or marketing effort; however, in some instances a low rate may be appropriate (in anticipation of rising prices and/ or shortages). A high turnover rate may indicate inadequate inventory levels, which may lead to lost opportunity for additional sales revenue.

An item whose inventory is sold (turns over) once a year has higher holding cost than that which turns more frequently; this ratio directly relates to the pace of sales. The purpose of increasing inventory turnover is threefold:

1. Increasing inventory turnover reduces storage costs; the firm spends less on rent, utilities, insurance, theft and other costs of maintaining stock.

2. Reducing holding costs increases profitability as long as the revenue remains constant.

3. Items that turn over more quickly increase the firm's responsiveness to changes in customer tastes.

High turnover may indicate that the inventory is too low, which may result in stock shortages.

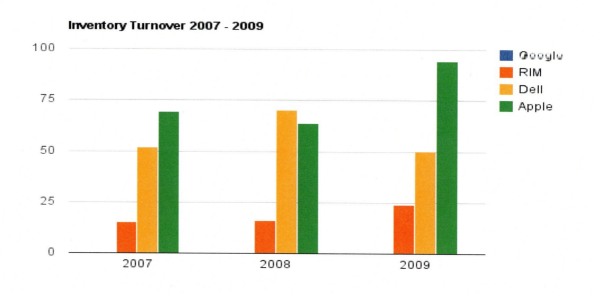

	Google	RIM	Dell	Apple
2007	n/a	15.17	51.81	69.38
2008	n/a	16.22	70.47	63.81
2009	n/a	24.06	50.33	94.30

The above chart is representative of the fact that Google does not sell a physical product.

The **accounts receivables turnover** ratio measures a company's effectiveness in the extension of credit and/ or collection of debt.

By maintaining accounts receivable, organizations are essentially extending interest-free loans to clients. A high ratio may imply that a company operates on a cash basis or that its extension of credit and/or its collection of accounts receivable is efficient.

A low ratio implies the company should re-assess its credit policies in order to ensure timely collection.

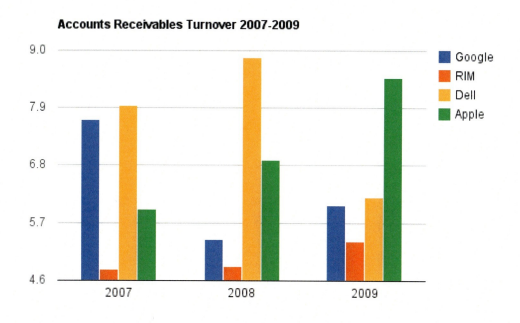

	Google	RIM	Dell	Apple
2007	7.67	4.81	7.95	5.96
2008	5.39	4.87	8.87	6.9
2009	6.05	5.34	6.19	8.48

Profitability Ratios

Net profit margin is a measure of profitability that is calculated by finding the net profit as a percentage of the revenue.

The profit margin is mostly used for internal comparison, and is difficult to accurately compare against different organizations. The operating and financing arrangements of firms vary greatly; different entities are bound to have different levels of expenditure. Thus, the comparison of one with another may have little meaning.

A low profit margin indicates a low margin of safety: higher risk that a decline in sales will erase profits and result in a net loss. Profit margin is also an indicator of a company's pricing strategy and how well it controls costs.

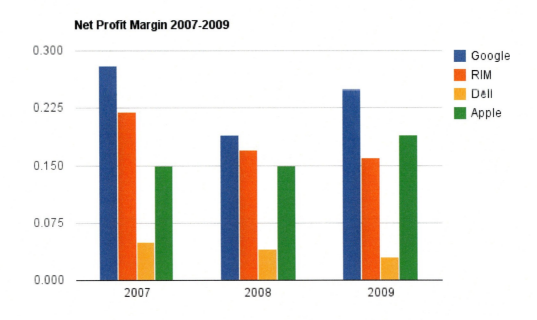

	Google	RIM	Dell	Apple
2007	.25	.22	.05	.15
2008	.19	.17	.04	.15
2009	.28	.16	.03	.19

Apple Inc

The **return on assets** (ROA) percentage shows how profitable a company's assets are in generating revenue. This ratio is useful in comparing competing firms within the same industry.

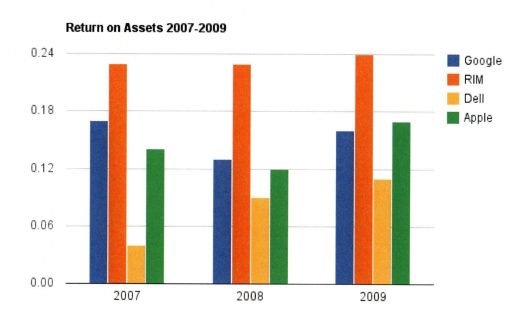

	Google	RIM	Dell	Apple
2007	.17	.23	.11	.14
2008	.13	.23	.09	.12
2009	.16	.24	.04	.17

Return on equity measures the rate of return on shareholders' equity, thus an organization's efficiency at generating profits from every unit of shareholders' equity. This measurement indicates how well a company uses investment funds to generate earnings growth.

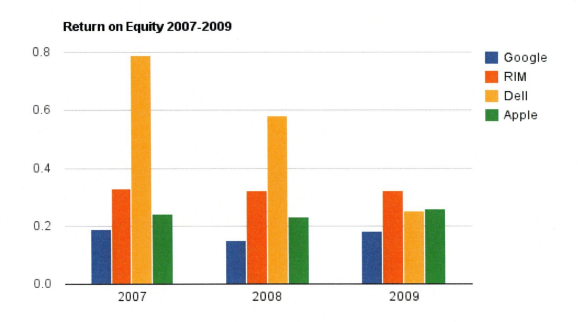

	Google	RIM	Dell	Apple
2007	.19	.33	.79	.24
2008	.15	.32	.58	.23
2009	.18	.32	.25	.26

Apple Inc

2. Altman Z-Score Analysis

The Z-score formula was published in 1968 by Edward I. Altman, an Assistant Professor of Finance at New York University.

The formula is used to predict the probability that a firm will go into bankruptcy within two years; the Z-score uses multiple corporate income and balance sheet values to measure the financial health of a company.

The original Z-score formula was as follows: $Z = 0.012T1 + 0.014T2 + 0.033T3 + 0.006T4 + 0.999T5$.

T1 = Working Capital / Total Assets. Measures liquid assets in relation to the size of the company.

T2 = Retained Earnings / Total Assets. Measures profitability that reflects the company's age and earning power.

T3 = Earnings Before Interest and Taxes / Total Assets. Measures operating efficiency apart from tax and leveraging factors. It recognizes operating earnings as being important to long-term viability.

T4 = Market Value of Equity / Book Value of Total Liabilities. Adds market dimension that can show up security price fluctuation as a possible red flag.

T5 = Sales/ Total Assets. Standard measure for sales turnover (varies greatly from industry to industry).

The Interpretation of Altman Z-Score:

Z-SCORE ABOVE 3.0 –The company is considered to be financially sound

Z-SCORE BETWEEN 2.7 and 2.99 – The firm is financially sound but demonstrates some areas of opportunity

Z-SCORE BETWEEN 1.8 and 2.7 – It is probable that the firm will go bankrupt within 2 years

Z-SCORE BELOW 1.80- High probability of imminent Bankruptcy.

Apple Inc

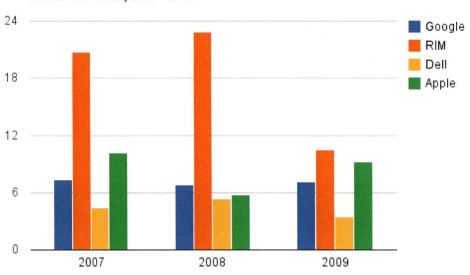

	Google	RIM	Dell	Apple
2007	7.29	20.77	4.37	10.15
2008	6.82	22.8	5.37	5.77
2009	7.13	10.49	3.44	9.22

3. Tobin Q Analysis

Tobin's Q is a ratio devised by James Tobin, who hypothesized that the market value of all the companies on the stock market should be about equal to their replacement costs.

The Q ratio is calculated as the market value of a company divided by the replacement value of the firm's assets

A low Q (less than 1) means that the cost to replace a firm's assets is greater than the value of its stock. This implies that the stock is undervalued.

Conversely, a high Q (greater than 1) implies that a firm's stock is more expensive than the replacement cost of its assets, which implies that the stock is overvalued.

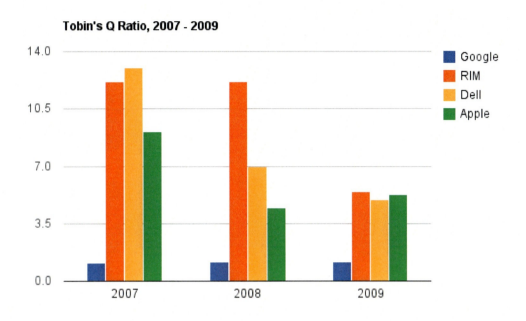

	Google	RIM	Dell	Apple
2007	1.07	12.14	13.00	9.08
2008	1.19	12.18	6.98	4.45
2009	1.14	5.45	4.97	5.28

DuPont Analysis

Apple

in millions...

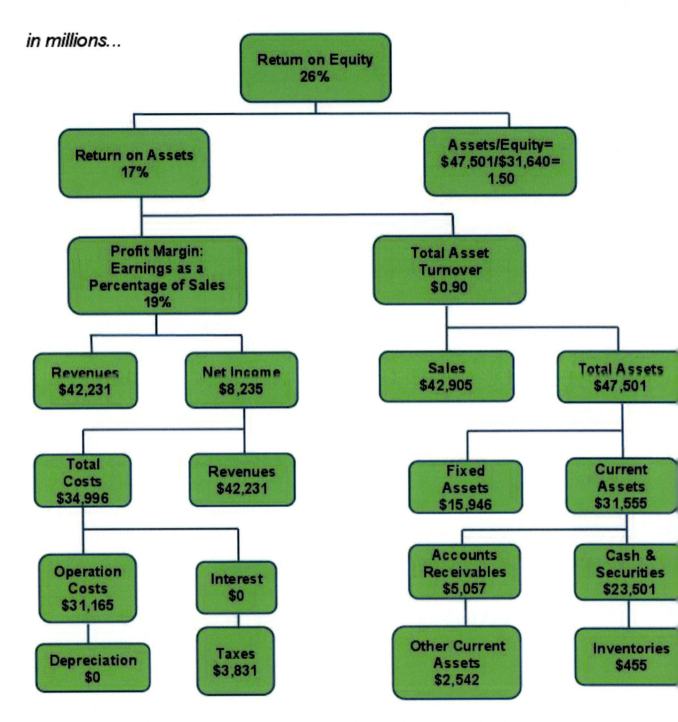

 Apple Inc

Google

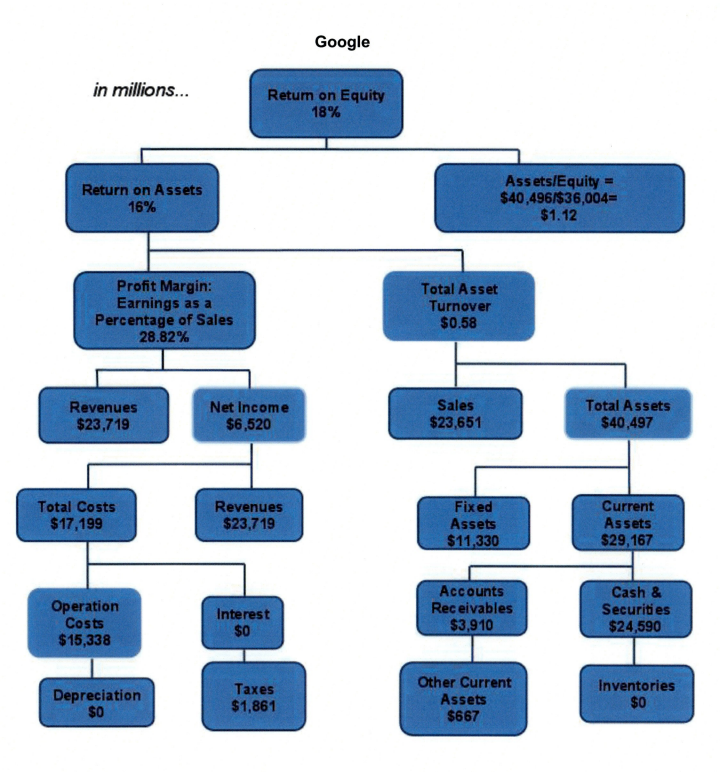

RIM

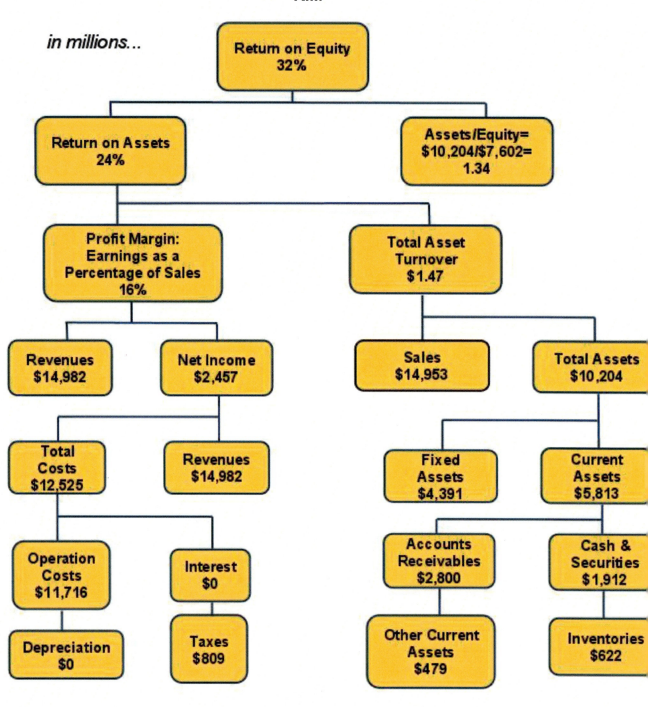

Dell

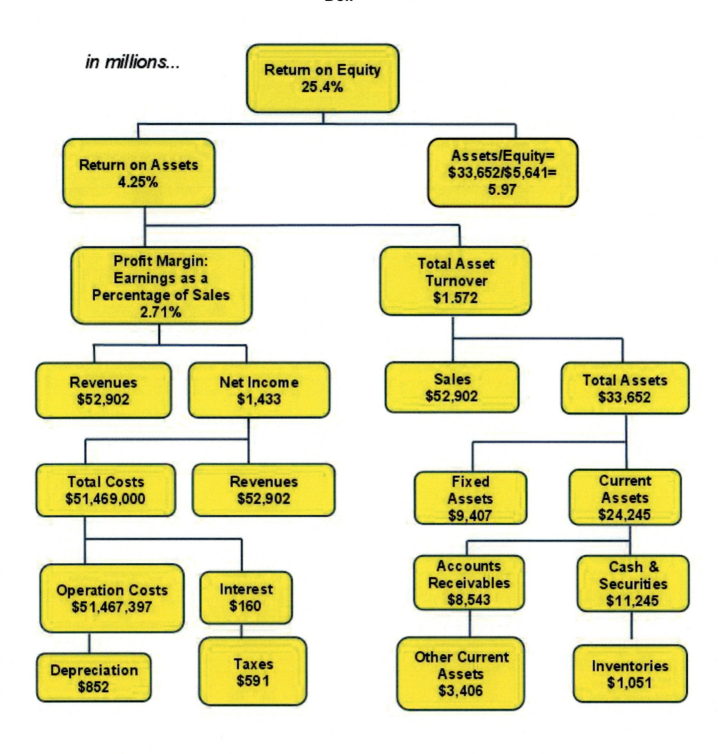

Apple Inc

I. SWOT Analysis

Strengths	Weaknesses
Strong Brand Image Robust Financial Performance Focused R&D Driving Innovation Extensive Product Offerings Convenient Customer Purchasing Broad Range of Applications for Products Strong Presence in Education Market Strong CEO, Steve Jobs No Long-Term Debt Leader in Employee Productivity Leader in Online Music Segment Brand Loyalty Cash-rich balance sheet - Low risk of bankruptcy Financial stability and performance improvement during an economic downturn	Product Recalls Patent Infringement CEO Succession New Product Release Issues New Technologies Cannibalizing Current Products Sales No Dividend Payment Portable Devices not Compatible with Adobe Flash iPhone and iPod Touch .pdf Security Issue Small global presence Relatively New to On-Demand Market
Opportunities	**Threats**
Strong growth in smart phones market segment Continuing Growth in Demand for Mobile PC's Expansion into other Mobile Carriers Lawsuits Involving other Competitors Increasing Demand for Tablet PCs in the Corporate Market Growing On-Demand TV Market Strong Growth in Asia/Pacific PC Market Search Engine for iPhone and iPod Integration of Technology into Modes of Transportation	Intense Competition Dependence on Specific Suppliers Economic Recession FCC Regulations Entry of New Competitors Product Substitution Strikes or Lockouts could Disrupt Manufacturing Capabilities Adverse Foreign Currency Exchange Rates Google Acquisition of Ad Mob

1. Strengths

Strong Brand Image
"The Apple brand is well recognized amongst most consumers. Apple's products enjoy a high level of brand awareness and brand recognition throughout all its markets. Moreover, the company's brand ranking, as per Interbrand, has been improving in recent years. Its brand ranking improved to 20th position in 2009 from 24 in 2008 and 35 in 2007. Apple's brand value improved to $15,433 in 2009 from $13,724 million in 2008 and $11,037 million in 2007.

Apple leverages its brand image to differentiate its product offering and drive sales. The company's strong brand enables it to command a premium pricing and create significant demand for its products such as iMac, iPod, iPhone and iPad. For instance, the company sold 300,000 iPads on the first day of its launch in the US in April 2010. Strong brand image gives the company an edge over regional competitors and other global competitors such as Sony."
("Datamonitor, *Apple, Inc.*" page 22)

Robust Financial Performance
"Apple reported robust financial performance in the past few years. The company's total revenue increased to $42,905 million in FY2009 from $24,578 million in 2007, representing a compounded annual growth rate (CAGR) of 32.1%. The company's operating income recovered from an operating loss in FY2003 to operating profits of $11,740 million, $8,327 million and $4,407 million, respectively, in FY2009, 2008 and 2007. As a result, the company's operating profit margin has improved to 27.4% in 2009 from 22.2% in 2008 and 17.9% in 2007. Following the trend, Apple's net income margin also improved to 19.2% in 2009 from 16.3% in 2008 and 14.2% 2007. Strong operating performance has resulted in higher cash from operating activities of $10,159 million in FY2009, compared to $9,596 million in 2008 and $5,470 million in 2007. Strong growth in revenues and cash flows indicates the company's robust financial position, which strengthens its investors' confidence, as well as allows it to invest in future growth avenues."
("Datamonitor, *Apple, Inc.*" page 22-23)

Focused R&D Driving Innovation
"Apple has a strong focus on research and development (R&D) as continual investment in R&D is critical for the development and enhancement of innovative products and technologies. In addition to evolving its PCs and related solutions, the company continues to capitalize on the convergence of the PC, digital consumer electronics and mobile communications by creating and refining innovations, such as the iPod, iPhone, iTunes Store, Apple TV and iPad. Apple leverages its unique ability to design and develop its own operating system, hardware, application software, and services to provide its customers new products and solutions with

superior ease-of-use, seamless integration, and innovative industrial design.

The company's R&D expenditure was $1,333 million, $1,109 million and $782 million in 2009, 2008 and 2007, respectively. The company's R&D spending is focused on further developing its existing Mac line of PCs, operating system, application software, iPhone and iPods. It also plans to develop new digital lifestyle consumer and professional software applications and invest in new product areas and technologies in coming years.

Apple's strong focus on research and development has led to the launch of innovative products such as iPod, iPhone and iPad enhancing its brand image and consolidating its market position."
("Datamonitor, *Apple, Inc.*" page 23)

"One other impressive feature of Apple's financial statements was that although the company had some minimal long-term debt in recent years, in February 2004 it retired the $300 million of outstanding debt (unsecured notes) it held, resulting in reporting long-term liabilities of $0. In retiring this debt, Apple did not deprive key operating areas of necessary levels of funding and much of Apple's operating budget was poured into research and development."
(Crafting and Executing Strategy, page C-150)

Extensive Product Offerings
Apple Inc. offers a wide range of products. They offer: desktop computers, lab-top computers, I-Pod, I-Pad, I-tunes, and I-Phone.

I-Macs are offered in 21.5-inch and 27-inch displays. Today's iMac has come a long way from the first 15-inch iMac. Take one look and you'll see just how far. A 21.5-inch or 27-inch display with edge-to-edge glass covers nearly the entire front of the enclosure. When all you see is the display, nothing gets between you and what's onscreen. Movies, TV show, websites, photos — everything looks stunning on the 16:9 widescreen iMac displays. The Computers has **LED backlighting.** When a display has more pixels, you need to push more light through them to achieve the best picture possible. LED backlighting in iMac does exactly that, with remarkable brightness and efficiency. Because the LED backlight doesn't take up much space, the iMac enclosure stays thin — even with all the high-performance components inside. They also have a **High resolution.** The 21.5-inch iMac features 1920-by-1080 HD resolution. Apple engineers could simply have stretched that resolution up and out for the 27-inch iMac. Instead, they took the display well beyond HD with 2560-by-1440 resolution. That's 78 percent more pixels than the 21.5-inch iMac. It also has **IPS technology.** The iMac display is designed to look great from almost any angle. A technology called in-plane switching (IPS) makes this possible. Whether you're sitting in front of the display or standing off to the side, you'll get a great picture with superb color

 Apple Inc

Apple offers three kinds of Notebooks are: MacBook, MacBook Pro, and Mac book Air. The MacBook is Apple's most affordable notebook. The MacBook Pro is their most advanced notebooks. The MacBook Air is the thinnest and lightest of the Mac   notebooks.

The iPad is a way Apple offers you the web, email, photos, and video. All of the built-in apps on iPad were designed from the ground up to take advantage of the large Multi-Touch screen and advanced capabilities of iPad. And they work in any orientation. So you can do things with these apps that you can't do on any other device.

The iPod's come in: the iPod Classic, iPod Touch, iPod Nano, and iPod Shuffle. The iPod classic gives you 160GB of storage capacity, good for up to 40,000 songs, 200 hours of video, 25,000 photos, or any combination. And you get up to 36 hours of battery
life, so you can keep on rocking for a long, long time. The iPod Touch uses face time, Retina display, HD video recording and editing, Game Center, Music, Movies, and TV shows. Face Time on iPod touch lets you hang out, catch up, and goof off with friends in an entirely new way. With just a tap, you can see what your friends are up to. The Retina display on iPod touch brings the highest-resolution iPod screen ever, with four times the pixel count of previous iPod models. The iPod touch has a HD video camera. The new Game Center app on iPod touch lets you add more players to your gaming network.

The iPhone 4 is more powerful, easier to use, and more indispensable than ever. It offers Face Time, Retina Display, Multitasking, HD Video Recording and Editing, 5-Megapixal Camera with LED Flash. The iPhone offers video calling with just a tap. iPhone 4 introduces a whole new way of multitasking. Now you can run your favorite third-party apps — and switch between them instantly — without slowing down the performance of the foreground app or draining the battery unnecessarily. The Retina display on iPhone brings the highest-resolution iPod screen ever, with four times the pixel count of previous iPod models. The iPhone has a HD video camera and take beautiful, detailed photos with the new 5-megapixel camera with built-in LED flash. The advanced backside illumination sensor captures great pictures even in low light. And the new front-facing camera makes it easy to take self-portraits.

iTunes is a free application for your Mac or PC. It organizes and plays your digital music and video on your computer. It keeps all your content in sync. And it's a store on your computer, iPod touch, iPhone, iPad, and Apple TV that has everything you need to be entertained. It can be accessed anywhere and anytime.

Convenient Customer Purchasing
Customers can purchase any of Apples products from the Apple website. The website is

Apple Inc

informative and can compare different products. Customers can also go to the iTunes website and download music, movies, and TV shows. Customers can go to any of these websites anytime and from anywhere.

Broad Range of Applications for Products
iPhones, iPod touch, and iPad has the capacity for using applications. You can download free or pay a small fee to get any app you wants. In the App Store you can find hundreds of thousands of apps designed for the iPhone, iPod touch, and iPad. The iTunes App Store is filled to the brim with quality entertainment apps (Marvel Comics, Netflix, Pandora Radio, Plants vs. Zombies HD), but there are also a number of apps that can help keep businesspeople productive when they're away from their primary computers.

Strong Presence in Education Market
Apple's key business marketing strategy in the company's early years was to market heavily on the educational market. Their assumption was, if students learned computer applications and techniques on Apple computers in school, they would demand Apple products in the business environment, therefore they could migrate their products through assimilation into the business environment. Although Apple was and is successful in penetrating the educational environment, the residual demand for their products in the business environment did not materialize. The development of Microsoft's "windows" interface made the conversion from Apple products to Microsoft based products relatively easy. Apple has become unable to effectively penetrate the business market.

Strong CEO, Steve Jobs
In the late 1970s, Jobs, with Apple co-founder Steve Wozniak, Mike Markkula and others, designed, developed, and marketed one of the first commercially successful lines of personal computers, the Apple II series. In the early 1980s, Jobs was among the first to see the commercial potential of the mouse-driven graphical user interface which led to the creation of the Macintosh. There was a power struggle with the board of directors in 1985, and Jobs resigned from Apple. Apple's subsequent 1996 buyout of NeXT brought Jobs back to the company he co-founded, and he has served as its CEO since 1997.

No Long-Term Debt

Apple Inc. every year makes a profit almost every year which allows them to show no long-term debt. This allows Apple, Inc. to have more opportunities than its competitors to invest in new technology or in research and development. There will be no worry regarding lack of capital for funding projects, whereas other competitors may have long-term debt that can potentially slow their process in research and development.

Leader in Employee Productivity

Apple is the leader employee productivity in their field. They strive to cut cost and have the highest possible production from their employees. Apple offers their employees the best possible benefits package as an incentive to encourage hard work and high productivity.

Leader in Employee Productivity

Apple has the highest productivity rate of its competitors. In 2009, Apple had a productivity rate of over $1.250 million per employee. That is 16.1% higher than RIM at $1.078 million per employee, 78.1% higher than Microsoft at $702,067 per employee, and 123% higher than Dell at $560,996 per employee.

Leader in Online Music Segment

Apple Inc. has been a leader in the online music segment since it introduced the iTunes Music Store in April, 2003. Since then, iTunes has sold more than 10 billion songs, according to a company announcement made in February 2010. In the first quarter of 2008, iTunes surpassed Wal-Mart Stores Inc. to become the largest music retailer overall in the US based on units sold, reported market research firm NPD Group (figures included online and retail sales, not mobile music sales). In 2009, iTunes accounted for 25% of all music sold in the US, up from 21 % in 2008 and 14% in 2007.

According to NPD, iTunes dominates the US digital music market, accounting for 69% of all songs
downloaded in the first half of 2009. Apple's online digital media shop, now known as the iTunes Store, has a catalog featuring more than 12 million songs, 55,000 TV episodes, and 8,500 movies (with 2,500 in high definition, or HD). In January 2009, the company announced that most of its music would be offered without copyright protection and with flexible pricing.

Brand Loyalty

Apple has successfully reinvented its' brand several time since the firm's inception. According to the book *the Brand Bubble,* this is precisely why consumers of Apple products are loyal.

Apple is lauded for its' ability to generate brand excitement and differentiation through innovation--the firm understands what the customer wants and subsequently provides. Unsuccessful firms assume that consumers will continue to purchase their goods and services because of brand awareness, not continuous growth, innovation, and development.

Apple Inc

2. Weaknesses

Product Recalls
"The company's products and services experience quality problems from time to time. Apple sells highly complex hardware and software products and services that can contain defects in design and manufacture. Defects may also occur in components and products that the company purchases from third parties. There can be no assurance the company will be able to detect and fix all defects in the hardware, software and services it sells.

For instance, in 2008, Apple announced Ultra compact USB Adapter Exchange Program. Under certain conditions, the new Ultra compact Apple USB power adapter's metal prongs broke off and remained in a power outlet, creating the risk of electric shock. Therefore, the company decided to exchange every Ultra compact power adapter for a new redesigned adapter, free of charge. Product defects may harm Apple's reputation and add significant warranty and other expenses."
("Datamonitor, *Apple, Inc.*" pages 23-24)

Patent infringement
"The company is involved in legal complaints relating to patent infringement. At the end of FY2009, the company was defending more than 47 patent infringement cases, of which 27 were filed in FY2009, and had several pending claims in various stages of evaluation. For instance, Nokia filed an action against Apple, in October 2009, in the US District Court for the District of Delaware, alleging the infringement of several US Patent that are essential to one or more of the GSM, UMTS and 802.11 wireless communications standards.

Unfavorable verdict in any of the matters related to patent infringement or other intellectual property rights will affect the company's financial condition and operating results."
("Datamonitor, *Apple, Inc.*" page 24)

CEO Succession
Steve Jobs' health has been a concern for some time; while Apple has said Jobs made a complete recovery from a rare form of pancreatic cancer following surgery in 2004, it hasn't stopped widespread speculation in the media, and may be impacting Apple's stock price.

Apple has yet to announce Jobs' successor, making some concerned about the future of the firm without its' dynamic leader.

New Product Release Issues

The iPhone 4 was released with several issues--most famous of which was a problem with reception. Specifically, the user's hand would unintentionally cover the handset's antenna given the device's design. This flaw and Apple's subsequent response damaged the firm's brand.

CEO Steve Jobs would later say in an exchange with a customer regarding the reception problems: "Non issue," the Apple chief executive told a Mac Rumors forumgoer via e-mail. "Just avoid holding it in that way."

No Dividend Payment

The absence of a dividend payment may push away possible investors.

Portable Devices Not Compatible with Adobe Flash

Apple and Adobe do not have a history of strong cooperation. The two firms engaged in a public dispute earlier this year when Steve Jobs posted a note on the Apple Web site that said Apple products would not include support for Flash because the technology is closed, unstable, and antiquated. Adobe responded by saying it would focus its attention on Android apps.

As of early September 2010, Apple had reversed course and said it would relax all restrictions on the development tools used to create iOS apps, as long as the resulting apps did not download any code.

"This is great news for developers and we're hearing from our developer community that Packager apps are already being approved for the App Store," Adobe said. "We do want to point out that Apple's restriction on Flash content running in the browser on iOS devices remains in place."

"Adobe will continue to work to bring full web browsing with Flash Player 10.1 ... to a broad range of devices, working with key industry partners including Google, HTC, Microsoft, Motorola, Nokia, Palm/HP, RIM, Samsung and others," the company said.

New Technologies Cannibalizing Sales of Current Products

With the increasing popularity of mobile computing, new technologies may cannibalize the sales of current products. The iPad has shown to be a very popular item and was considered to take away sales of competitor's net books. However, sales analysts are reducing their estimates of low-end MacBook sales. In contrast, a thinner MacBook air is expected to be released which may take away sales from the iPad.

Apple Inc

iPhone & iPod Touch .pdf Security Issue
By loading certain PDF files onto your iPhone or iPod Touch could cause problems. This can give access to "hackers" to your handheld. When a user loads a PDF document, it has to load the fonts associated with it. Then what is called a stack overflow will be inserted. This result means that the handheld security defenses will be broken and can cause critical damage to your phone. It is very similar to the Jailbreak me website and its process.

Small Global Presence
"Apple has been losing some market share to Android, Google's rapidly growing operating system, but the iPhone is still special." A world mobile phone market share graph by Brand shows that Nokia owns 40% of the market share globally while Apple comes in at 2%. Samsung is next with 20% of the market share globally. "Apple is being dominated globally by Nokia, the global leader, and Samsung and LG. However, Apple dominates all of them, RIM's BlackBerry included, in terms of value share. Despite its relatively smaller presence in the world, Apple owns Nokia, Samsung, LG and BlackBerry combined in terms of revenue for smart phones. When it comes to market share, it seems that the numbers don't mean a whole lot in terms of profitability."

Relatively new to on-demand market

Although Apple TV has been around since 2007, Apple emphasized that the product was an accessory to iTunes and a Mac/PC. The product needed to be connected to a PC to work and would only work with content streamed or purchased form iTunes. Apple released an update that would later make Apple TV a standalone box. However, it would still only show content from iTunes and not from other sources such as Netflix, Amazon.com and Blockbuster. Other devices such as TiVo, Nintendo's Wii, and Microsoft's Xbox were already a standalone box that can stream content from multiple sources.

3. Opportunities

Strong Growth in Smartphone's Market Segment
"The worldwide smart phones market segment is forecast to record strong growth in coming years. The worldwide smart phones shipments, which accounted for about 15% of worldwide mobile phones shipments in 2009, are forecast to account for over 35% of shipments in 2012. The demand for worldwide touch-screen devices is forecast to almost double in 2010 and will account for more than half of total mobile phones shipments in 2013.

Apple became the third largest player in the Smartphone market segment in 2009 since launching its first mobile device, iPhone, in 2007. iPhone is a multimedia and internet-enabled

mobile phone, combining mobile phone, widescreen iPod and internet functionalities and applications that support email, web browsing and maps on a mobile phone. It is available in 80 countries distributed through various channels. The iPhone has additional features such as multi touch display and related software. The company also experienced strong growth in its iPhone business in recent years. Its iPhone and related offerings revenues almost doubled, at a rate of 93.3% in 2009 over 2008, to record revenues of $13,033 million. With its innovative products such as iPhone, Apple is in a position to increasing its share of the growing smart phones market segment."
("Datamonitor, *Apple, Inc.*" page24)

Continuing Growth in Demand for Mobile PCs
"The worldwide mobile PCs market segment is forecast to record strong growth in coming years. In 2009, the mobile PCs shipments, which include sales of laptops, notebooks, net books and tablet PCs, grew by more than 15% over 2008, while the desktop PCs shipments declined. The growth in mobile PCs was mainly due to increase in consumer market demand. Further, the mobile PCs shipments are forecast to record a CAGR of 19% during 2009–14. This growth was above the overall PC market growth of CAGR of 12% during the same period, signifying strong growth in the segment. The growth in this market is expected to be driven by demand from both developed and developing nations.

Apple is one of the top five leading players in the mobile PCs market segment. Moreover, the company has been enhancing its portfolio to take advantage of the growing mobile PC market with enhancements for existing products and launch of new products. Further, in April 2010, Apple launched its iPad, a high-resolution, Multi-Touch display device for browsing the web, reading, sending email, and viewing entertainment content with responsive, and sold 300,000 iPads on the first day of its launch in the US.

Strong growth outlook for the mobile PCs market segment will create demand for the company's products in coming years."
("Datamonitor, *Apple, Inc.*" pages 24-25)

Expansion into other mobile carriers
"Analyst predicts that Apple's iPhone sales figures will grow by 27 percent per year in 2010 and 2011. They note that Apples expansion to other mobile carriers will help grow their sales figures, they think that by offering the iPhone on the Verizon network in the US will increase sales to them by as much as 11 million new sales. With expansion into other parts of Europe and in China that number will easily hit 50 million."

Lawsuits involving other competitors
Apple has been very aware of the Apple patents that it owns. Over the past few months, Apple

Apple Inc

has been suing companies over patent infringement. "Apple is using its strong patent portfolio to fight iPhone competitors in court." "Apple thinks it owns the concept of the touch screen Web phone and it wants other cell phone makers to pay for copying the iPhone or to stop altogether." Steve Jobs was quoted in a press release saying: "We can sit by and watch competitors steal our patented inventions, or we can do something about it. We've decided to do something about it. We think competition is healthy, but competitors should create their own original technology, not steal ours." Apple will be able to generate income through these lawsuits if deemed the winner. Other companies will have to start all over if deemed the loser.

Increasing Demand for Tablet PCs in the Corporate Market
Apple has always been an innovator when it has come to technology, and one area where they are was again raising the bar has been with their version of the tablet PC called the IPAD. In the first two months the IPAD was on the market, over 2 million units were sold in the United States. The IPAD has the opportunity to replace laptops in the corporate market. The IPAD performs all the major functions that a corporate business person needs and so much more.

Growing On-Demand TV Market
An emerging market that has formed over the past several years has been the On-Demand TV market. Gone are the times where families would drive to the video store for a movie night. Gone are the times where couples would stop at the video store after a date. Technology now allows us to watch new movies as well as old ones through our TV's, video game systems, and computers. Most of the major video store chains have all gone under, most recently was Blockbuster in August of 2010. The Apple TV is beginning to tap into this market that has endless possibilities.

Strong Growth in Asia/Pacific Market
An emerging market on the global scale is the Asia/Pacific market especially in the Smartphone industry. Shipments in the region are expected to grow 53% year-on-year in 2010 to reach 76.7 million units and are projected to easily surpass 100 million units in 2011. Furthermore, Canalys forecasts that APAC will overtake Europe, the Middle East and Africa (EMEA) in 2012 to become the largest regional smart phone market, accounting for 36% of global shipments. Apple is also forecast to grow significantly this year. In 2009, APAC was its fastest growing region with 261% year-on-year growth. 'Apple had a good 2009 in APAC, overcoming several big challenges,' said Lau. 'Unlike in North America where the iPhone is firmly established, in APAC Apple has had to deal with countries dominated by domestic brands, such as Japan and South Korea, where international vendors have historically struggled, combined with its relatively weak brand strength in certain country markets in the region. It achieved strong growth last year as it rose to these challenges. Expect to see continuing significant growth for Apple in the quarters and years ahead as it establishes itself

in new markets and addresses pent-up demand, helped undoubtedly by the announcement of the iPhone 4.' Canalys expects Apple volumes to grow 90% in 2010 to 9.1 million units, making it the second largest OS vendor in the region.

Search Engine for iPhone and iPod
Google is the default search engine for the iPhone and iPod Touch. As Apple and Google become more competitive with each other, this leaves Apple's iPhone and iPod app data vulnerable for review by Google. Google sees what iPhone users are searching for, which can help it tailor software and services for its own mobile smart phones.

Integration of Technology into Modes of Transportation
Technology has become an integral part in modes of transportation. Whether by land, sea or air technology can be seen throughout. The biggest advance has been in the last few years with Microsoft producing Sync to be used in Ford vehicles. Sync allows the users of the Ford vehicles to listen to their zune or cell phone devices using the car audio system. This presents an opportunity for Apple to develop software to be used in automobiles where the IPhone and IPad can be used. Since Apple wants to enter the Asian market a logical choice would be to partner with either Honda or Toyota.

4. Threats

Intense Competition
"Apple operates in a highly competitive and rapidly evolving technology industry. The company faces intense competition in consumer electronics, PCs and related software and peripheral products markets. Rapid technological advances in both hardware and software, increasing the capabilities and use of PCs and digital electronic devices, characterize these markets. Rapid changes in the technology have resulted in the frequent introduction of new products with competitive prices, features and performance characteristics.

The company's competitors include Microsoft, Dell, Hewlett-Packard, Fujitsu, Samsung Electronics, Sony and Toshiba, among others. The company is currently focused on market opportunities related to mobile communication devices including the iPhone. The mobile communications industry is highly competitive with several large, well-funded and experienced competitors. Further, the launch of iPhone spiked the demand for Smartphone with touch functionality and other innovative features. This made several players in the mobile phone market, such as Nokia, HTC, RIM, Palm, Samsung and LG Electronics, launch their respective Smartphone devices in the market creating significant competition. Intense competition in various markets in which Apple operates could result in the price erosion which may affect the

 Apple Inc

company's revenues and profitability in the long run." ("Datamonitor, *Apple, Inc.*" page 25)

Recently, Apple has launched the iPad tablet. Dell, HP, Samsung and RIM have begun launching tablet products. Some of these tablets come in smaller sizes while others are similar in size to Apple's with varying prices to match.

Dependence on Specific Suppliers
"The company depends on third party suppliers for various components used in its products. In case of PCs, Apple sources most of the general components from multiple sources and certain key components from single or limited customers. These key components include DRAM, NAND flash-memory, and TFT-LCD flat-panel displays. The company also uses certain customized components from single source, which are not generally used by the other PC manufacturers. Further concentration of manufacturers on the production of components other than those needed by Apple will also affect its supply. Lack of suppliers for key components, will adversely affect the company's operations."
("Datamonitor, *Apple, Inc.*" pages 25-26)

Economic Recession
The current economic recession has caused chip makers to scale back production of the chips necessary to build smart phones. While Apple hasn't reported problems with the supply of chips from its suppliers there have been problems reported with chips being supplied to cellular communication providers to upgrade their equipment. Data capacity on these networks may not expand quickly enough to accommodate the increase in iPhone sales.

FCC Regulations
Apple provides many products that communicate via wireless method and, therefore, must comply with FCC regulations. New products must be submitted to the FCC before release to obtain approval and regulations can change to accommodate new standards in wireless communication. Changing standards can have an impact on current production causing the manufacturer to halt production until changes can be made to the product.

Entry of New Competitors
A threat of new competitors is a threat to almost all IT companies. There is a huge level of competition in the technology markets and Apple is no different than any other company in this respect. Whenever you are successful like Apple is, it will attract competition. Apple is a company that works extremely hard on research and development. They have a very successful marketing department as well that helps them retain their competitive position.

Product Substitution
A few years ago CD's dominated the market. Now our attention has turned to iPod's and MP3

players. Tomorrow's technology might be completely different. Wireless technologies could replace the need for a physical music player.

Strikes or Lockouts Could Disrupt Manufacturing Capabilities
The workforce in China, and other Asian countries, is becoming more assertive and selective, and sometimes inclined to protest by strikes, slow-downs and, most often, quitting. China, as an example, has had strikes originate mainly from their migrant labor force. Younger migrant workers are becoming more demanding about job conditions. They see their futures in the cities, not in farming, and feel the pressure to save up money despite rising costs. They are also gaining more bargaining power as the flow of potential job seekers tightens, because of wider opportunities and fewer entrants into the workforce as the population ages. But rising overall costs, and the risk that strikes could force sudden jolts in wage levels, could prompt more companies to move production to and from different parts of China or to other Asian countries causing a major disruption in production capabilities.

Google Acquisition of Ad Mob
Ad Mob provides Google with the ability to serve display ads, the pictorial banners that are the chief revenue source for most Web sites, to cell phones and other mobile devices. Owning Ad Mob stands to make Google and its Android software more enticing to advertisers that seek a wide audience and developers eager for part of a market expected to surge more than eightfold to $1.78 billion in 2014. Ad Mob received 2.6 billion ad requests from iPhone and iPod touch devices in September [2009], up from 130 million in September '08. (It received 10.2 billion total requests in September.) With this acquisition, Google will have access to information supplied by apps on the iPhone and iPod Touch.

Search Engine for iPhone and iPod
Google is the default search engine for the iPhone and iPod Touch. As Apple and Google become more competitive with each other, this leaves Apple's iPhone and iPod app data vulnerable for review by Google. Google sees what iPhone users are searching for, which can help it tailor software and services for its own mobile Smartphone.

Adverse Foreign Currency Exchange Rates
The foreign currency exchange rates can greatly affect US companies doing business around the world. Companies can lose money if the value of the currency is low or high. The rates could work in favor of a company or greatly hinder their ability to do business.

Apple Inc

a. TOWS Matrix

TOWS Matrix for Apple, Inc.	INTERNAL STRENGTHS	INTERNAL WEAKNESSES
	Strong Brand Image Robust Financial Performance Focused R&D Driving Innovation Extensive Product Offering Convenient Customer Purchasing Broad Range of Applications for Products Strong Presence in Education Market Strong CEO, Steve Jobs No Long-Term Debt Leader in Employee Productivity Leader in Online Music Segment Brand Loyalty	Product Recalls Patent Infringement CEO Succession New Product Release Issues New Technologies Cannibalizing Current Product Sales No Dividend Payments Portable Devices not Compatible with Adobe Flash iPhone & iPod Touch .pdf Security Issue Small Global Presence Relatively New to On-Demand Market Low Asset Turnover
EXTERNAL OPPORTUNITIES	**STRENGTHS OPPORTUNITIES**	**WEAKNESSES OPPORTUNITIES**
Strong Growth in Smartphone's Market Continuing Growth in Demand for Mobile PCs Expansion into other Mobile Carriers Lawsuits Involving other Competitors Increasing Demand for Tablet PCs in the Corporate Market Growing On-Demand TV Market Strong Growth in Asia/Pacific PC Market Integration of Technology into Modes of Transportation	S - Focused R&D Driving Innovation O - Strong Growth in Smartphone's Market *Market Penetration - Expand Smartphone capabilities and market S - Focused R&D Driving Innovation O - Continuing Growth in Demand for Mobile PCs *Market Penetration - Expand Mobile PC Market and Capabilities S - Strong Brand Image O - Expansion into other Mobile Carriers *Market Development - Offer iPhone and	W - Product Recalls O - Strong Growth in Smartphone's Market O - Continuing Growth in Demand for Mobile PCs O - Expansion into other Mobile Carriers O - Increasing Demand for Tablet PCs in the Corporate Market O - Growing On-Demand TV Market O - Strong Growth in Asia/Pacific PC Market *Innovation - Learn from Past Recalls to Avoid Future Recalls W - New Technologies Cannibalizing

Apple Inc

	iPad to other Mobile Carriers S - Extensive Product Offering O - Increasing Demand for Tablet PCs in the Corporate Market *Market Development - Market iPad for Corporations S - Broad Range of Applications for Products O - Integration of Technology into Modes of Transportation *Concentric Diversification - Integrate Technology into Automobiles and Airplanes	Current Product Sales O - Growing On-Demand TV Market *Horizontal Integration - Expand into On-Demand Market W - Small Global Presence O - Strong Growth in Asia/Pacific PC Market *Market Development - Expand into Asia/Pacific Market W - Relatively New to On-Demand Market O - Growing On-Demand TV Market *Joint Venture - Joint Venture with On-Demand Provider
EXTERNAL THREATS	STRENGTHS THREATS	WEAKNESSES THREATS
Intense Competition Dependence on Specific Suppliers Economic Recession FCC Regulations Entry of New Competitors Google - Acquisition of Ad Mob Product Substitution Strikes or Lockouts Could Disrupt Manufacturing Capabilities Adverse foreign currency exchange rates Search Engine for iPhone and iPod	S - Focused R&D Driving Innovation T - Intense Competition *Innovation - Develop New Ideas to Stay Ahead of Competition S - Strong Brand Image T - Entry of New Competitors T - Product Substitution *Market Penetration - Focus on Marketing of Current Products to Scare New Entrants S - Robust Financial Performance T - Google Acquisition of Ad Mob *Concentric Diversification - Use Large Cash Balance to Purchase Online Ad Company S - Strong Presence in Education Market T - Drop in Computer Demand *Market Development - Expand Deeper into the Education Market S - Leader in Online Music	W - Patent Infringement T - Entry of New Competitors *Horizontal Integration - Purchase Competitor to Reduce Possibility of Infringing on Patents T - Small Global Presence W - Economic Recession *Market Development - Expand into Growing Asia/Pacific Market W - Patent Infringement T - Dependence on Specific Suppliers *Backward Vertical Integration - Purchase Parts Suppliers to Control Quality and Reduce Infringement

Apple Inc

| | Segment
T - Entry of New Competitors
*Market Penetration - Vigorously Market iTunes Music Store to Hinder New Entrants
S - Focused R&D Driving Innovation
T - Search Engine for iPhone and iPod
*Innovation - Create Robust Search Engine | |

II. Focal Points for Action
A. Short Range

- Partner with additional carriers
- Market Apple TV and innovate on-demand products
- Have a succession plan for top executives especially CEO
- Increase global presence with worldwide retail stores openings
- Create new alliances with companies in our industry to expand the international market.
- Enter the Online advertising
- Produce tablet-style PCs

B. Long Range

- Develop technology to combat music piracy
- Regulate future patent proceedings
- Continue developing new products
- Revolutionize desktop computers and lap-tops
- Develop an Apple based search engine

III. Develop Alternatives

A. Consider Generic Industry Type

Apple currently offers products that fits into multiple industries. Domestically, the computer and peripheral industry is expected to have a negative growth rate over the next five years. The development of computing capabilities in other products, such as cell phones, will generate competition resulting in further decline. However, portability will be a factor in driving growth for some products. Business demand could also be stimulated by the replacement of old computers and peripherals with newer technology. Globally, the industry is expected to grow at a compounded annual growth rate of 5.9% from 2008 - 2013 suggesting that Apple focus on global markets.

The communication equipment industry is expected to have a near flat growth rate over the next five years, domestically. This industry is losing out to manufacturers located in counties located outside the United States. These manufacturers have lower costs and can be more competitive on cost per unit. Firms will be cutting unprofitable lines and focusing on fewer, higher margin products. More firms will be outsourcing manufacturing and applying more capital to research and development and marketing. Globally, this industry is expected to grow at a compounded annual growth rate of 6.7% between 2008 and 2013 with the Asia-Pacific segment holding the largest share at 51.7% suggesting Apple focus on the Asia-Pacific market.

Apple Inc

B. Boston Consulting Group Matrix

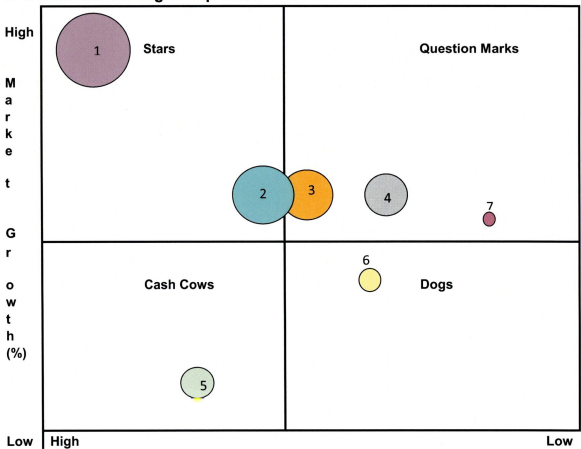

1. iPhone SIC 3575
2. Portables SIC 3575
3. iPod SIC 3575
4. Desktop SIC 3571
5. Music SIC 3572
6. Software SIC 3572
7. Peripherals SIC 5045

C. Competitive Position

Industry	Position
Computer & Peripheral Manufacturing in the U.S NAICS 33411 **Desktops, Peripherals, & Other Hardware** Companies in this industry manufacture and/or assemble personal computers, mainframes, workstations, laptops and computer servers. Industry participants may also manufacture computer storage devices that allow the storage and retrieval of data from a phase change, magnetic, optical or magnetic/optical media.	Follower
Communication Equipment Manufacturing 33422 **iPhone** This industry includes firms engaged in manufacturing radio and television broadcast and wireless communications equipment. Examples of products made by these firms are: transmitting and receiving antennas, cable television equipment, GPS equipment, pagers, cellular phones, mobile communications equipment, and radio and television studio and broadcasting equipment.	Challenger
Computer Manufacturing in the U.S NAICS 33411a **Portables & iPod Industry** Companies in this industry manufacture, design or assemble personal computers (PCs), laptops, handheld computers and servers. Industry operators typically purchase computer components (e.g. graphics cards and motherboards) from dedicated manufacturers in other industries (see report 33441a – Semiconductor & Circuit Manufacturing). Manufacturers of computer monitors, mice, keyboards and printers are covered in 33411b – Computer Monitor and Peripheral Manufacturing.	Leader
Computer Stores in the U.S NAICS 44312 **Apple Store and iTunes Store** Desktop computers, notebook computers, and software are the key focus of this industry. Computer stores also provide a range of accessories like printers,	Leader

scanners, and keyboards. These goods are purchased from domestic and international manufacturers and wholesalers and then sold to stores. Consumers purchase the majority of goods supplied by this industry for private use, while businesses purchase a small share of goods.	
Software Publishing in the U.S. NAICS 51121 Software publishers carry out operations necessary for producing and distributing computer software, such as designing, providing documentation, assisting in installation and providing support services to software purchasers. These firms may design, develop and publish, or publish only. Industry works are often passed on to reproduction manufacturers of optical media in order to mass-produce copies of the original software program/application.	Follower

D. Competitive Strategy Options

Porter's Model for Apple

	Broad	Narrow	
Low Cost			1. 33411 Computer & Peripheral Manufacturing in the U.S. 2. 33422 Communication Equipment Manufacturing 3. 33411a Computer Manufacturing Portables and iPod 4. 44312 Computer Stores in the U.S. Apple Store, iTunes Store 5. 51121 Software Publishing in the U.S.
Differentiated	1 2 3 4 5		

*

Rivalry among competing sellers in the industry

SIC 33411 - *Moderate*	SIC 33422 - *Strong*
• Medium Concentration • Negative Growth Rate • Brand names are important in this industry to diversify competitors	• There are many competitors in the smart phone segment • Companies that continually innovate, such as Apple, will remain ahead • Levels of competition is high

Apple Inc

SIC 33411a - *Strong*	SIC 44312 - *Strong*
<ul><li>Concentration in this industry is high</li><li>Apple continually innovates its products</li><li>Apple is an effective advertiser creating stronger growth</li></ul>	<ul><li>Concentration in this industry is high</li><li>Expertise of staff on various products is high</li><li>Consumers are price sensitive and will shop around</li><li>Competition is intense in this industry</li></ul>
SIC 51121 - *Moderate*	
<ul><li>Level of concentration is medium</li><li>Innovation is important for product differentiation</li><li>Switching costs are high</li><li>Industry is growing</li></ul>	

Potential entry of new competitors

SIC 33411 - *Weak*	SIC 33422 - *Moderate*
<ul><li>Barriers to entry are high</li><li>Regulation is low</li><li>Expectation of retaliation by incumbents is low</li><li>Loyalty is moderate</li><li>Loyalty to Apple is moderate</li></ul>	<ul><li>Technology is similar; patent infringement is high</li><li>Barriers to entry of this industry are high but declining</li><li>Outsourcing possibilities reduce entry costs</li></ul>
SIC 33411a - *Strong*	SIC 44312 - *Weak*
<ul><li>Barriers to entry are low</li><li>Threat of retaliation by incumbents is high</li></ul>	<ul><li>High level of competition</li><li>Concentration is high</li><li>Regulations are low</li></ul>

SIC 51121 - *Moderate*

- Competition is high
- Regulation is low
- Concentration is medium
- Industry is growing

Competitive pressures from substitute products

SIC 33411 - *Strong* • Cell phones, MP3 players, and digital TVs can incorporate the functions of PCs • Substitute products can be substantially lower in price	**SIC 33422** - *Strong* • Many different cell phones offer similar functions
SIC 33411a - *Strong* • Technology among competitors is similar • Buyer is not necessarily price sensitive	**SIC 44312** - *Strong* • Suppliers can offer products directly to consumers • More suppliers can vertically integrate by opening their own stores
SIC 51121 - *Weak* • There are many products that offer the same functionality • Switching cost can be high	

Apple Inc

Competitive pressures from supplier bargaining power

SIC 33411 - *Weak*	SIC 33422 - *Weak*
• Chip makers have a low concentration level • Apple has a high dependence on certain suppliers	• Chip makers have a low concentration level • Apple has a high dependence on certain suppliers
SIC 33411a - *Weak*	SIC 44312 - *Weak*
• Chip makers have a low concentration level • Apple has a high dependence on certain suppliers	• Suppliers need an outlet for their products • Supplier may lack distribution channels of their own • High concentration in this industry means few choices for product placement
SIC 51121 - *Strong* • Integral relationship with 3341 industry hardware needs software and vice-versa • Switching cost is high • Supplier concentration is medium	

Competitive pressures from buyer bargaining power

SIC 33411 - *Weak* • Buyers in this industry are fragmented • Many substitute products exist • Apple has opened many of its own stores and sells direct to the public through its website	SIC 33422 - *Weak* • Cell phones are available through carriers • Switching cost to end user is low
SIC 33411a - *Weak* • Buyers in this industry are fragmented • Many substitute products exist • Apple has opened many of its own stores and sells direct to the public through its website	SIC 44312 - *Strong* • Customers are price sensitive and will shop around • Ability to substitute is strong but declining • Cost to customer to switch is low
SIC 51121 - *Weak* • Buyers are fragmented • Switching costs are high • Firms can forward integrate by opening their own retail outlets	

E. Rumelt's Criteria

Apple RUMELT'S CRITERIA

Strategy	Consistency	Consonance	Feasibility	Advantage	Total
Market Penetration					
Expand Smartphone capabilities and market	5	5	5	5	20
Expand Mobile PC Market and Capabilities	5	5	5	5	20
Focus on Marketing of Current Products to Scale New Entrants	4	3	5	5	17
Vigorously Market iTunes Music Store to Hinder New Entrants	5	4	5	5	19
Market Development					
Offer iPhone and Pad to other Mobile Carriers	4	5	5	5	19
Market Pad for Corporations	3	5	3	3	14
Expand into Asia/Pacific Market	3	5	5	5	18
Expand Deeper into the Education Market	4	3	5	4	16
Innovation					
Develop New Ideas to Stay Ahead of Competition	5	5	5	5	20
Learn from Past Recalls to Avoid Future Recalls	4	3	5	4	16
Create Robust Search Engine	1	3	1	1	6
Concentric Diversification					
Use Large Cash Balance to Purchase Online Ad Company	2	3	4	3	12
Integrate Technology into Automobiles and Airplanes	1	4	1	2	8
Horizontal Integration					
Expand into On-Demand Market	4	5	5	5	19
Purchase Competitor to Reduce Possibility of Infringing on Patents	2	4	2	2	10
Backward Vertical Integration					
Purchase Parts Suppliers to Control Quality and Reduce Infringements	2	3	2	3	10
Joint Venture					
Joint Venture with On-Demand Provider	1	5	3	5	14

Apple Inc

IV. Decisions & Recommendations

A. Corporate

Mission Statement

It is Apple's mission to help transform the way people work, learn and communicate by providing exceptional computing and innovative customer service. We will pioneer new directions and approaches finding innovative ways to use computing technology to extend the bounds of human potential. Apple will make a difference: our products, services and insights will help people around the world shape the ways business and education will be done in the 21st century." Apple's mission statement details its strategic position to achieve profitability and the competitive advantage. Apple's strategic position is to give users the best computing experience by innovating in hardware, software, and Internet offerings

Strategic

- Continue expansion into Asian markets. This includes but is not limited to continuing to grow and market the IPhone as well as continue to open Apple stores.
- Market the IPhone and iPad on more than one carrier. Currently the IPhone and iPad are on the AT&T network. Having the devices on multiple carriers provides a new customer base and allows Apple to compete with other competitors who are on multiple networks
- Continued development of Apple TV
- Continue to be an innovation leader. Apple has hit it big with innovations of the iPod, IPhone, and iPad all because of being a leader in technological innovation. Apple cannot be afraid to take a chance on the next bright idea.

Financial

- Increase revenue 5% to 7% a year over the next 5 years
- With the expansion of more apple stores, generate an increase in sales for our iPod and peripheral divisions
- Gain mobile contracts to carriers other than AT&T. IPhone sales were up 93% for 2009. If the IPhone was carried on other providers, Apple should increase the 2009 sales by 50%
- Maintain stock price of $300

- Elimination of the desktop computer division. Sales were down 23% in 2009 and will not be helped with more marketing of iPad

B. Business
Computers

Objectives:
- Increase sales of iPad
- Increase sales of laptops
- Gain deeper acceptance of iWork in business and education
- Reduce inventory of Desktop computers

Strategies:
- Update iPad operating system and develop additional applications
- Make laptops customizable and special order
- Address incompatibilities between iWork and Microsoft Office
- Integrate broadband capabilities into laptops
- Pursue video and content production communities
- Make Desktop computers a special order items

Online media/applications

Objectives:
- Gain broader market penetration in software development
- Gain broader market penetration of On Demand Market

Strategies:
- Market small to medium business solutions
- Increase funding to software development
- Launch Apple TV

Apple Stores

Objectives:
- Increase store sales of third party accessories by 10%
- Increase sales of OSX to existing Apple owners

Strategies:

Apple Inc

- License the sale of Apple apparel to department stores
- Open additional apple stores in South America and Asia with the focus in China
- Offer a wide range of products

C. Functional
Finance

- Increase revenues 5% to 7% over 5 years.

Research & Development

- Create a program to recycle old Apple products.
- Production facilities developing more useful ways to improve technology.
- Improve technology through R&D.

Information Technology

- Update the functionality of our website.
- Use our website to implement a search for Apple stores.
- Improve the capabilities of our website.

Ethical Practices

- Practice ethics in order to maintain operations in international and domestic markets.
- Develop an ethics committee to ensure proper ethical measures are being taken.
- Have "green" committees come in to talk to employees about ways to promote social responsibility.

Operational Focus

- Have a good corporate strategy.
- Instill a solid corporate culture.
- Continue to inspect production lines.

Human Resources

Apple Inc

- College credit Program, Interns can attain college credits by working for apple and completing course work for school. This will be beneficial for them to gain knowledge of the business environment as well as get college credits.
- Keep employees satisfied with current post-retirement plans.
- Use employee satisfaction surveys to better understand what your employee's needs and wants.

Marketing

- Develop the Apple brand internationally.
- Be competitive in the market with keeping costs low.
- Grow by acquiring companies with a good strategic fit.

V. Implementation

Goal: Expand Smartphone capabilities and market
Participants: Marketing, iPhone Engineering, VP of iPhone Software
Steps:

- Build relationship with other carriers such as Verizon and U.S. Cellular
- Establish engineering program to create new capabilities and open iPhone to other carriers' technology
- Develop marketing campaign to focus on new features of iPhone

Goal: Expand mobile PC market and capabilities
Participants: Marketing, Portables Engineering, VP of Portables
Steps:

- Build relationship with educational facilities and major corporations
- Develop portable capabilities for the healthcare industry
- Develop marketing campaign to focus on features of iPad and iPod Touch

Goal: Vigorously Market iTunes Music Store to hinder new entrants
Participants: Marketing, VP of Music Relations
Steps:

- Establish an agreement with as many record labels as possible
- Focus on establishing a relationship with EMI records to sell Beatles music
- Give away ten free downloads with every $100 purchase with Apple
- Place iTunes gift cards in all grocery, book, and convenient stores
- Create a rewards program that awards points based on the number of downloads

Apple Inc

Goal: Expand into On Demand market
Participants: Marketing, VP Devices Hardware Engineering, Research and Development
Steps:

- Establish central data server providing on demand content
- Partner with Amazon.com and Hulu
- Partner with major cable and satellite carriers for combo device

Goal: Expand into Asia/Pacific market
Participants: Marketing, CEO, COO
Steps:

- Establish relationship with mobile carriers in the Asian market
- Open Apple Stores in India and more stores in China

VI. Citations

United States. Securities and Exchange Commission. *Form 10-K Apple Inc.* , 2009. Web. 8 Oct 2013.
<http://www.sec.gov/Archives/edgar/data/320193/000119312509214859/d10k.htm>

Datamonitor. *Apple, Inc Company Profile.* 21 May 2010. 1 September 2010
<http://web.ebscohost.com.ezproxy.lewisu.edu/ehost/>

Datamonitor. "Dell, Inc. Company Profile." *EBSCO HOST*. Datamonitor, 8 July 2009. Web. 1 Oct. 2010.

Datamonitor. "Google, Inc. Company Profile." *EBSCO HOST*. Datamonitor, 9 July 2010. Web. 1 Oct. 2010.

Datamonitor. "Research In Motion Company Profile." *EBSCO HOST*. Datamonitor, 27 Aug. 2010. Web. 1 Oct. 2010.

Apple, Inc. *Corporate Governance Guidelines.* 27 May 2009. 1 October 2010
<http://www.apple.com/investor/>

Apple, Inc. *Audit and Finance Committee Charter.* 26 May 2009. 1 October 2010
<http://www.apple.com/investor/>

Apple, Inc. *Compensation Committee Charter.* 27 May 2009. 1 October 2010
<http://www.apple.com/investor/>

Apple, Inc. *Nominating and Corporate Governance Committee Charter.* 27 May 2009. 1 October 2010
<http://www.apple.com/investor/>

Graph - http://www.socialstudieshelp.com/Eco_Business_Structures.htm

Lovero, Dr. Eveann. "Organizational Structures." Strategic Management 59-620-1. 2010. Page 645-664

Lovero, Dr. Eveann. "Chapter 4 Financial Ratios." *Strategic Management 59-620-1*. 2010. Print. Page 104.

"Current Ratio." *Wikipedia, the Free Encyclopedia*. Web. 16 Nov. 2010.
<http://en.wikipedia.org/wiki/Current_ratio>.

Thomson, Jr., Arthur A., A.J. Strickland III, and John E. Gamble. *Crafting and Executing Strategy, The Quest for Competitive Advantage, Concepts and Cases*. 17. New York, NY: McGraw-Hill Irwin, 2010. C-150. Print.

MarketingTeacher.com. Swot Analysis Apple.
http://www.marketingteacher.com/swot/apple-swot.html

Gerzema, John, and Ed Lebar. "The Brand Bubble." *Dtcperspectives.com*. Robert Ehrlich, June 2009. Web. 3 Nov. 2010.
<http://www.dtcperspectives.com/content/editor/files/June2009/PerspectivesonBooks-TheBrandBubble.pdf>.

Staff, MacNN. "Fortune: Who Is next Apple CEO, Jobs' Successor? | MacNN." *Apple, Macintosh, IPad, IPod and IPhone News | MacNN*. 24 June 2008. Web. 03 Nov. 2010. <http://www.macnn.com/articles/08/06/24/fortune.steves.successor/>.

Newman, Jared. "4 Easy Answers to IPhone 4 Problems - PCWorld." *Reviews and News on Tech Products, Software and Downloads - PCWorld*. 26 June 2010. Web. 03 Nov. 2010. <http://www.pcworld.com/article/199928/4_easy_answers_to_iphone_4_problems.html>.

Albanesius, Chole. "Adobe Resumes Work on IPhone Flash Tool After Apple Reversal | News & Opinion | PCMag.com." *Www.pcmag.com*. 10 Sept. 2010. Web. 03 Nov. 2010. <http://www.pcmag.com/article2/0,2817,2368965,00.asp>.

"Mobile Operating System." *Wikipedia, the Free Encyclopedia*. Web. 05 Nov. 2010. <http://en.wikipedia.org/wiki/Mobile_operating_system>.

" List of Mobile Network Operators." *Wikipedia, the Free Encyclopedia*. Web. 05 Nov. 2010. <http://en.wikipedia.org/wiki/List_of_mobile_network_operators>

Zwolak, Roman. "IBISWorld Industry Report 51322 Cable, Internet& Telephone Providers in the US." *IBISWorld*. Sept. 2010. Web. 7 Nov. 2010.

"Geert Hofstede." *Wikipedia, the Free Encyclopedia*. Web. 13 Nov. 2010. <http://en.wikipedia.org/wiki/Geert_Hofstede>.

Geert Hofstede Cultural Dimensions. Web. 13 Nov. 2010. <http://www.geert-hofstede.com/>.

Baldoni, John. "Wanted: Inspirational Leaders - John Baldoni - Harvard Business Review." *Business Management Ideas - Harvard Business Review Blogs*. 16 Mar. 2009. Web. 13 Nov. 2010. <http://blogs.hbr.org/baldoni/2009/03/wanted_inspirational_leaders.html>.

Disclosure Incorporated, comp. "APPLE INC Disclosure SEC Database." *Disclosure Online Database*. LexisNexis, 11 Oct. 2010. Web. 14 Oct. 2010.

Disclosure Incorporated, comp. "DELL INC Disclosure SEC Database." *Disclosure Online Database*. LexisNexis, 11 Oct. 2010. Web. 14 Oct. 2010.

Disclosure Incorporated, comp. "GOOGLE INC Disclosure SEC Database." *Disclosure Online Database*. LexisNexsis, 25 Oct. 2010. Web. 27 Oct. 2010.

Disclosure Incorporated, comp. "RESEARCH IN MOTION LTD Disclosure SEC Database." *Disclosure Online Database*. LexisNexis, 11 Oct. 2010. Web. 14 Oct. 2010.

Articles, TV | More. "Will Apple Stay on Top in the Tablet Wars? (AAPL, AMZN, DELL, HPQ, MOT, MSFT)." *Fool.com: Stock Investing Advice | Stock Research*. 2 Oct. 2010. Web. 4 Oct. 2010. <http://www.fool.com/investing/general/2010/10/03/will-apple-stay-on-top-in-the-tablet-wars.aspx>.

Letzing, By John. "Microsoft Takes Retail Challenge to Apple's Door - MarketWatch." *MarketWatch - Stock Market Quotes, Business News, Financial News*. 5 Oct. 2010. Web. 7 Oct. 2010. <http://www.marketwatch.com/story/microsoft-takes-retail-challenge-to-apples-door-2010-10-05>.

Kane, Yukari I., and Miguel Bustillo. "Laptop Sales Sapped by Tablet Frenzy - WSJ.com." *Business News & Financial News - The Wall Street Journal - WSJ.com*. 5 Oct. 2010. Web. 7 Oct. 2010. <http://online.wsj.com/article/SB10001424052748704789404575523800740263636.html>.

Baetz, Juergen | More. "Germany Warns Apple Products Face Security Threat." *Manufacturing.net*. 4 Aug. 2010. Web. 11 Oct. 2010. <http://www.manufacturing.net/News/2010/08/Electrical-Electronics-Germany-Warns-Apple-Products-Face-Security-Threat/>.

Butcher, Dan. "Will Apple Launch Its Own Search Engine to Thwart Google? - Mobile Marketer - Search." *Mobile Marketer - The News Leader in Mobile Marketing, Media and Commerce*. 6 Apr. 2010. Web. 5 Oct. 2010. <http://www.mobilemarketer.com/cms/news/search/5886.html>.

Boulton, Clint. "Apple May Build a Search Engine to Shield IPhone Data from Google - Search Engines - News & Reviews." *Technology News, Tech Product Reviews, Research and Enterprise Analysis - News & Reviews*. 4 Apr. 2010. Web. 5 Oct. 2010. <http://www.eweek.com/c/a/Search-Engines/Apple-May-Build-a-Search-Engine-to-Shield-iPhone-Data-From-Google-705980/>.

Hoff, Rob. "Google Buys AdMob in Bid to Boost Mobile Ads - BusinessWeek." *BusinessWeek - Business News, Stock Market & Financial Advice*. 9 Nov. 2010. Web. 10 Oct. 2010. <http://www.businessweek.com/the_thread/techbeat/archives/2009/11/google_buys_adm.html>.

Parr, Ben. "Security Exploit Can Give Hackers Control of Your IPhone or IPad [WARNING]." *Social Media News and Web Tips – Mashable – The Social Media Guide*. 1 Aug. 2010. Web. 15 Oct. 2010. <http://mashable.com/2010/08/03/iphone-pdf-exploit/>.

Schonfeld, Erick. "Apple Goes After HTC In Lawsuit Over 20 IPhone Patents." *TechCrunch*. 2 Mar. 2010. Web. 15 Oct. 2010. <http://techcrunch.com/2010/03/02/apple-goes-after-htc-in-lawsuit-over-20-iphone-patents/>.

Thormahlen, Casey. *IBISWorld Industry Report 33411 Computer and Peripheral Manufacturing in the US*. Rep. IBISWorld, 2010. *IBISWorld*. Web. 1 Oct. 2010.

Thormahlen, Casey. *IBISWorld Industry Report 33411a Computer Manufacturing in the US*. Rep. IBISWorld, 2010. *IBISWorld*. Web. 1 Oct. 2010.

Fitzpatrick, Nigel. *IBISWorld Industry Report 33422 Communication Equipment Manufacturing in the US*. Rep. IBISWorld, 2010. *IBISWorld*. Web. 1 Oct. 2010.

Thormahlen, Casey. *IBISWorld Industry Report 44312 Computer Stores in the US*. Rep. IBISWorld, 2010. *IBISWorld*. Web. 1 Oct. 2010.

Thormahlen, Casey. *IBISWorld Industry Report 51121 Software Publishing in the US*. Rep. IBISWorld, 2010. *IBISWorld*. Web. 1 Oct. 2010.

Datamonitor. *Global Communications Equipment Industry Profile*. Rep. no. 0199-2024. Datamonitor, 2009. *EBSCO HOST*. Web. 1 Oct. 2010.

Datamonitor. *Global Computers and Peripherals Industry Profile*. Rep. no. 0199-2027. Datamonitor, 2009. *EBSCO HOST*. Web. 1 Oct. 2010.

Apple, Inc. *Apple Supplier Code of Conduct*. Cupertino: Apple, Inc., 2010. PDF.

Made in the USA
Middletown, DE
07 November 2017